RESCUE
FROM
GRAMPA WOO

RESCUE
FROM
GRAMPA WOO

Joan Skelton

Natural Heritage Books

Rescue from *Grampa Woo*
Joan Skelton

Natural Heritage / Natural History Inc.
P.O. Box 65, Station O,
Toronto, Ontario, M4A 2M8

Cover and Text Design by Steve Eby
Edited by Jane Gibson

Printed and bound in Canada by Hignell Printing Limited, Winnipeg, Manitoba.

Canadian Cataloguing in Publication Data

Skelton, Joan
    Rescue from Grampa Woo
Includes bibliographical references and index.
ISBN 1-896219-45-4

1. Rescues — Superior, Lake. 2. Grampa Woo (Ship). 3. Glenada (Ship).
I. Title.
VK1323.7.S53 1998   363.12'381'0971312   C98-931869-9

THE CANADA COUNCIL | LE CONSEIL DES ARTS
FOR THE ARTS | DU CANADA
SINCE 1957 | DEPUIS 1957

Natural Heritage / Natural History Inc. gratefully acknowledges the support received for its publishing program from the Canada Council Block Grant program. We also acknowledge with gratitude the assistance of The Association for the Export of Canadian Books, Ottawa.

dedicated to those who work to protect the Lake
and to my Mother

TABLE OF CONTENTS

1 ~ THE BEGINNING 1

This is Nature—the balance of colossal forces.

2 ~ THE EIGHTH SEA 13

Each blade of grass has its spot on earth whence it draws its life, its strength.

3 ~ THE WOMEN IN HIS LIFE 37

The marital relations of seamen would make an interesting subject, and I could tell you instances ...

4 ~ HER SOUL ENCODED BY WATER AND BOATS 54

This sea and this sky were open to me...there was a sign, a call in them—something to which I responded with every fibre of my being.

5 ~ THE CREWS AND THE SHIPS 73

We exist only in so far as we hang together.

6 ~ GRAMPA WOO 90

It was as if I had jumped into a well—into an everlasting deep hole.

7 ~ THE LONGEST HOUR 104

It is all in being ready.

The blight of futility that lies in wait for men's speeches had fallen upon our conversation, and made it a thing of empty sounds.

Man is amazing, but he is not a masterpiece.

This wonder; this masterpiece of Nature.

ACKNOWLEDGEMENTS

Rescue from Grampa Woo would not have been written without Germaine Kangas asking me to write the story. In Toronto at the time, my husband Stan and I were delayed and confounded by a storm as we tried to drive home. Little did we know it would become known as "the *Grampa Woo* storm." Outside Sault Ste. Marie, we were engulfed in a blizzard, and at our cottage past the Sault, we found a gigantic old-growth spruce felled in the driveway; the steps to the beach, some sixty feet from the waterline, torn out. Having witnessed the *Fitzgerald* storm, having seen an ocean-vessel beached by the *Socrates* storm, I was not surprised there were some navigational repercussions, but eight people in three little boats surviving a storm of such magnitude? Germaine's phone call suggesting I write the story piqued my interest. Captain Gerry Dawson and the others involved captured it.

Captain Dawson, his family, Captain Dana Kollars, Chief Coxswain Bob King, the crew of the *Glenada*, *Westfort*, and *Grampa Woo*, in general the waterfront scene, cooperated with a great deal of honesty and patience. As with Germaine, without them, *Rescue from Grampa Woo* would not have been written. In particular, I would like to thank Gerry Dawson and Inga Thorsteinson who provided unstinting information, advice, and help. Too, I would like to thank Jim Harding, Jack Olson, Willie Trognitz, and Robin Sivill, who, with Gerry, Bob, Inga, and Dana, all met the storm and lived to tell me about it with candour and emotion.

In the forefront of the background was Sharon and Wealthy Dawson who lent a special insight to the story. Ed Greer, ChunAe Kollars, and the Dawson children, Nathan, Heather, and Davis, deserve a special mention. On the waterfront in various parts of the Lake were: *Chief Shingwauk's* Captain Frank Prouse of Sault Ste. Marie;

Twolan's Captain Stan Dawson; Lieutenant Randall Wagner of United States Coast Guard, Duluth, Minnesota; Gene Onchulenko; Captain Fred Broennle; Superintendent Douglas Barnard of Isle Royale National Park, Michigan; Thunder Bay Waterfront Commissioner Dennis Johnson; Captain Jack Gurney; Captain Roger Hurst; all who generously agreed to be interviewed, many of whom were photographed. Eila and T. Virene and Ruth and Werner Beyer shared with me their experience of a seiche.

Superintendents Laurie LaChapelle and Brian Palmer of Marine Communications and Traffic Services, Sarnia, Ontario; Greg Sladics, Canadian Coast Guard, Trenton, Ontario; Don Murray, District Manager, Thunder Bay/Kenora, Ministry of Environment and Energy; Alexander Paterson, N.M. Paterson & Sons, Thunder Bay; Gail Jackson, Parks Canada, Thunder Bay, Ontario; Anne Plouffe, Fisheries and Oceans, Ottawa; Joyce Mortimer, Health Canada, Ottawa; John Africano of American Steamship Company, Williamsville, New York; James Danielson, regional representative, Fort William First Nation; Jake Vander Wal, manager, and Jim Bailey and Ed Iwachewski of Lake Superior Programs, Thunder Bay, Ontario; Marie Hales, Minnesota Sea Grant; Paula Davidson, Lake Superior Center; Shawn J. Allaire of InfoTech Services; Denis O'Hare, John Futhey, Vi Thompson, Rose Bava, all were most cooperative, as were the office staffs of Stan Dromiski, MP, and Joe Comuzzi, MP. Oceanographer Dr. Michael McCormick, Ann Arbor, Michigan, answered my internet plea for help with Lake Superior water temperatures. Primary Foto Source produced quality processing.

In the literary and writing community, Christina Stricker of Sweet Thursday Bookshop, Elinor Barr of Singing Shield Productions, Bill MacDonald of Fireweed, and Penny Petrone and Charles Wilkins each helped in their own special way.

In the media, Gary Rinne, news director of CHFD-TV, Richard Boone of CKPR, the Chronicle Journal, *Soundings*, TVOntario and Sleeping Giant Productions, and Minnesota Sea Grant Extension allowed use of their material.

Lyyli Kangas and Doris Arnold generously provided interview space. Jim Harding, as part of his computer company, All-Tech Services, created the charts of the rescue and the refuge. Justice John Wright corresponded with me on e-mail about heroes. Kathy Hunt of MediScribe designed the invitations to the launching sponsored by the Navy League of Canada, Thunder Bay Branch, and H.M.C.S. Griffon, with thanks to President Maria Lassonde and Lieutenant Commander Keith Dawe. Waverly Resource Library Reference Department helped with my research and documentation. Nancy Erickson read the manuscript. All made a great contribution.

Photographs were entrusted to me by Gerry and Sharon Dawson, Wealthy Dawson, Gail Jackson, Mike Jones, Dana and ChunAe Kollars, Gene Onchulenko, Inga Thorsteinson, Lieutenant Randall Wagner, and T. and Eila Virene.

Of great importance was the support of my husband, Stan, whose enthusiasm for my writing, and his all-too-honest critiques of my manuscripts, always provides just what a writer needs.

Barry Penhale of Natural Heritage Books was both courteous and incisive during the final crush of editing.

And, to the Lake—Lake Superior—for being there. Many thanks.

AUTHOR'S NOTES

Rescue from Grampa Woo is the factual, authorized version of a real life drama on Lake Superior. With the cooperation of the families, crews, the Canadian and United States Coast Guards and the *Access to Information Act*, much of the story is told through the words of the people involved. The fifty or more face-to-face interviews conveyed so much honesty, emotion and unexpected eloquence, the words simply demanded to be quoted.

All references and quotations are credited in the "Notes" at the back of the book, beginning on page 157. Unless otherwise indicated, the remarks were made to me, to Germaine Kangas and me, or to Germaine in the three interviews she conducted alone. It was Germaine that drew the story to my attention and asked me to write about it. We worked together on the early research. My fascination grew. Each day the story became more compelling and refreshing, more archetypal in its proportion.

Some inconsistencies in the stories are inevitable. These were not corrected. Who can say whose perception was correct about the exact height of the waves on *that night*, October 30, 1996? Even under the best circumstances, it is difficult to measure waves objectively. Perceptions vary slightly, not only of fact but also about events and time. Every attempt was made to search out the accurate story and time-frame, even to the point of invoking *Access to Information* procedures to get data from the Canadian Coast Guard radio log. The log was especially useful regarding time, so easily distorted by distance, danger, and activity.

However, *Rescue from Grampa Woo* is not investigative journalism per se. The story of each individual was taken pretty well at face value; its veracity stands in the recounting of each individual's perception.

The head-note of each chapter is taken from *Lord Jim* by Joseph Conrad. Those who know the book will see the similarities with *Rescue from Grampa Woo*. They are both sea stories; both involve calamity; both involve a need for decision.

There is also great contrast. Jim always dreamed of being a hero. Gerry was just doing his job. Jim was young, away from home, and with no back-up or support from his family or crew. Gerry was a settled man, with psychological support from his wife and family, and physical, almost intuitive, back-up from his crew. In the *agony of collision*—a legal phrase expressing the crisis point of decision—Jim was not ready: he jumped. Gerry was ready: he stayed.

Both men were haunted by the incident. One to his death.

Steep-sided wave.

Lake Superior vista.

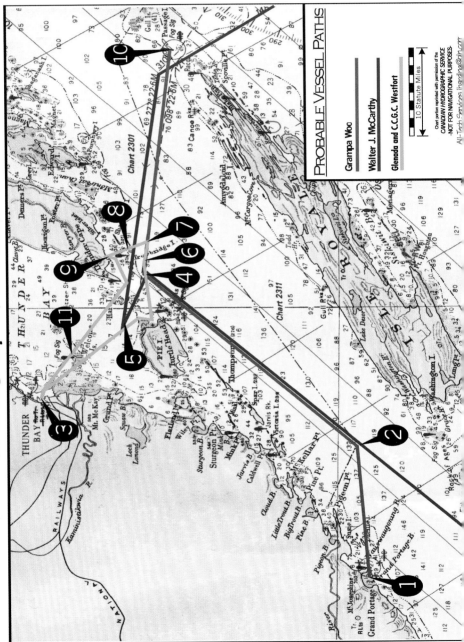

EVENTS OF THE RESCUE

PROBABLE VESSEL PATHS

Grampa Woo

Walter J. McCarthy

Glenada and C.C.G.C. Westfort

10 Statute Miles

Chart portion reprinted with permission of the
CANADIAN HYDROGRAPHIC SERVICE
- NOT FOR NAVIGATIONAL PURPOSES

All-Tech Services lhardina@in.com

Chart of route of rescue.

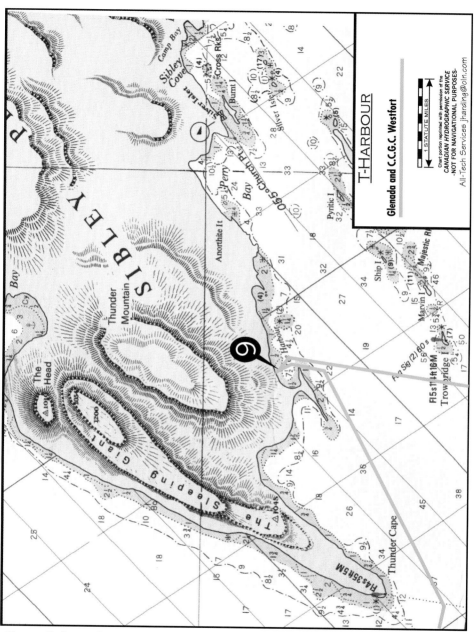

Chart of place of refuge: Tee Harbour.

Day One: October 30, 1996

1. *Grampa Woo's* mooring adrift, 8:00 am.
2. *Walter J. McCarthy Jr.* takes *Grampa Woo* in tow, 2:34 pm.
3. *Glenada* and *Westfort* leave Thunder Bay harbour, 4:30-5:00 pm.
4. Towing bridle parts and *Grampa Woo* adrift again, 6:49 pm.
5. *McCarthy* seeks shelter.
6. *Glenada* tries to get *Grampa Woo* in tow.
7. *Glenada* pulls two men off, 8:04 pm.
8. *Glenada* and *Westfort* head for shelter at Tee Harbour.

Day Two: October 31, 1996

9. *Glenada* and *Westfort* storm-stayed at Tee Harbour.
10. United States Coast Guard finds *Grampa Woo* shipwrecked on Passage Island.

Day Three: November 1, 1996

11. *Glenada* and *Westfort* return home, 1:30 pm.

The Sleeping Giant floats on a bed of mist across from Thunder Bay harbour, one of the many optical illusions that occur on Lake Superior.

1 ~ THE BEGINNING

This is nature—the balance of colossal forces.

The man hugged himself for warmth and reassurance as he sat on an ancient beach of Lake Superior, now Hillcrest Park in Thunder Bay. He sipped coffee while the snow and wind swirled around him. He stared into the dizzying grey. Occasionally, the light of the setting sun behind him penetrated through the squalling snow to the Lake. He leaned forward and stared harder, but could see nothing.

"What else could he do?"[1]

Two wives, strangers to each other and 130 miles apart, consoled each other by phone. A mother, who knew only too well the worries of a mariner's wife, busied herself with an injured grandson and did not hear the news. Nor did her family tell her.

A city watched and listened. An astute phone call to the Canadian Coast Guard from a country music radio reporter, routinely checking on possible consequences of the storm, exploded into a chain reaction between newsrooms. Both Canadian and American newsrooms were scrambling.

Five men and one woman, "six miles from the closest land,"[2] were fighting their human frailty as their two vessels struggled to pluck two stranded mariners from the unpredictable malevolence of a propellerless cruise ship, unsteady with ice and swaying broadside in the turbulent sea of Lake Superior. *Grampa Woo* had broken its mooring at Grand Portage, Minnesota. Although 110 feet long and built for the Atlantic, it was reduced to helplessness.

1

For four hours and fifteen minutes it had been in tow by the downbound lake freighter, *Walter J. McCarthy, Jr.*, a thousand foot ore carrier owned by American Steamship Company and riding low with a load of coal for St. Clair, Michigan.[3] *Grampa Woo* was being hauled northwards some 29 miles (25 nautical miles) towards the shelter of Thunder Bay, hauled with all the peculiarity of an elephant dragging a Gainsborough.

As the *McCarthy* veered westward towards Thunder Bay harbour, the towing bridle parted, broke, in a fetch—a stretch—of unprotected water. Again, the tour boat was loose, carrying away its helpless former masters, the Captain and his crewman, fortunately the only ones aboard.

The *McCarthy* and another nearby thousand footer, the *Oglebay Norton*, left the floundering ship. They knew that somewhere nearby were a tug and a Coast Guard cutter. Those vessels would have to take over. The Lake that sank the 729 foot *Edmund Fitzgerald* now was sending two 1000 foot lakers heading for shelter.

Standing by was the *Glenada*, hired while *Grampa Woo* was in tow. The *Glenada* was to take over from the

Walter J. McCarthy, Jr., ore carrier, one thousand feet in length.

McCarthy inside the protection of the greater harbour of Thunder Bay and tow *Grampa Woo* to safe dockage. The Canadian Coast Guard Search and Rescue vessel, *Westfort,* was tasked to assist. Forty-four feet long and only 25 tons, it was a ping pong ball by Lake Superior standards. The tug *Glenada* was sturdier at 76 feet and 107 tons.

Both had been waiting in the lee of Turtlehead, the wind-lashed headland that is the southern portal of the greater harbour of Thunder Bay. In open water, waves were 15 to 18 feet and building in a typical Lake Superior west by north-west cross-wind. It was a beam sea, the ships taking the wind at right angles to their direction, taking it broad-side. Snow and ice were obscuring visibility. All was black except for the pinpricks of running lights, the darting of searchlights, and the white manes of the sea. It was the early dark of the night before Halloween.

"Usually when something rotten happens, it's going to happen in the worst possible conditions. Blowing gales, snow, rain and dark, too. Hardly ever do you see something happen in the day-time for some reason."[4]

Eight lives were in jeopardy. Three were in the round-bellied *Westfort,* designed for the rolling salt water swells of the ocean, not the steep, erratic waves of Lake Superior. It was tipping almost to right angles, sluggish from snow and ice, taking on water in its buoyancy chamber. Once, its Chief Coxswain, its captain, radioed the ship was going over. Its blip on the *Glenada's* radar screen disappeared. Its radio transmissions ceased.

"The waves went from eight feet to 12 feet and then they went to 18 feet and then they went to 20. The whole rescue event took place in those horrific winds and everything was moving at about four and-a-half to five knots."[5]

"It was black and wild and insane."[6]

Another three in jeopardy were on the private enterprise tug boat, the *Glenada*. Below, the engineer was sick from diesel fumes, noise, and the punches of unseen waves. Nervously he watched the half cup of water in the glass bowl of the Raycor filter on the fuel feed-line. This water could kill the rescue operation and likely the crew.

"The truck came down and brought a load of contaminated fuel which had about 150 or 200 gallons of water and sludge—and we got it in our fuel tank. We worked all afternoon, three or four hours. In the meantime, there's all kinds of water hung up in your pipes. So you get all the fuel clean but all the sludge stays right in the bottom, and then you get out in the storm that we were in and it gets all mixed up and you start getting it back in your engine again—just mixes it up like you were stirring a soup. So that was the concern. You can lose pretty near anything, but if it's the engine, boy, you got nothing left. That's it."[7]

On deck, the lone crewman of the *Glenada*, sliding and sloshing around with a rope and pike pole, was trying to heave a line to *Grampa Woo*.

"There was enough water on the back deck at the time to float my legs. I was holding onto the tow post and you know, my legs would lift up and start sucking up into one of the scuppers. Way too much fun. The wind would start to climb up and then it would crash down on the back deck. I found myself chortling back there and I know that's my stressor reactor. I start to chortle and I know then that I'm way too stressed about something."[8]

His hands were freezing to the heaving line as he tried to throw. At times his orange floater suit was freezing him to the ship. The Captain kept trying to manoeuver the *Glenada* into position for his crewman to throw a rope to the captives on *Grampa Woo*.

The tug, *Glenada*, riding low in the water.

"I was holding on for dear life and then having the heaving line freeze to me every time I decided to throw it. It was just wild. I mean the pitching and blowing and the dark was nuts."[9]

The *Glenada* meanwhile was dodging a maelstrom of waves and the 150 feet of rope dangling from *Grampa Woo*, another threat to its engines.

In the back of the Captain's mind was the image of the *McCarthy* heading towards shelter after the towing bridle broke. Three city blocks in length, almost a fifth of a mile long, it was ten times the size of the other ships.

"The *McCarthy* could have provided lee for us and I still to this day don't know why he didn't."[10]

As the *Glenada* struggled with a line for *Grampa Woo*, its Captain thought his deckhand had gone overboard. The crewman was worried too.

"I remember thinking on the back deck of my son and I can't...I'm not allowed to go over the side...too many responsibilities...trying to get the line...I mean there was no way I was going over...I just refused to go over the side...it just wasn't going to happen."[11]

At the same time the *Glenada's* Captain thought the crewman had gone over, he also thought the *Westfort* had capsized. The *Westfort's* Chief Coxswain also had concerns.

"There was times when our boat was rolling 80 to 90 degrees, laying our ship right on her side. At one point, I said I think we are going to go over."[12]

The Captain of the *Glenada* believed he was alone. His hand was bleeding from scraping an envelope-size hole in the frosted windshield, his only porthole in the cocooning ice. What could he do? He turned away from the wobbling *Grampa Woo* to look for his crewman and to collect his thoughts.

He had three major worries: his crewman was floundering about somewhere in the black of the waves; the *Westfort* had capsized with three flung into the water; and a propellerless cruise ship with two men aboard was being swept away.

The Captain of the *Grampa Woo* also had major worries. The lights from the *Glenada* had disappeared and the last radio broadcast from the *Westfort* indicated it may have capsized. He too felt alone. Abandoning ship was the only option for him and his crewmen. He issued a public broadcast for help.

"He radioed that his situation was dire and must abandon ship."[13]

On the *Glenada*, the Captain heard the tapping of a pike pole on a side window. His crewman was safe. He learned his crewman had been struggling to inch away from the stern, awash with a knee-deep boarding sea, towards the forward deck where the footing was treacherous with ice from freezing spray. Finally able to respond to the Captain's shouting on the intercom, the crewman sidled into a position where his taps on the window could be heard over the storm. With the re-appearance of the crewman, one major worry was gone.

Radio transmissions resumed from the *Westfort* and the Captain knew it had not capsized. Another major worry was gone.

But more developed. The Captain learned his engineer was so sick he had to retire to his bunk. There was no-one in the engine room; no-one to watch the filter for water from the bad fuel. The sea was continuing to build. The ships were continuing to ice from freezing spray.

Nevertheless, the *Glenada* turned back towards the floundering *Grampa Woo*.

The two exhausted and hypothermic men were relieved to see the lights of the *Glenada* re-appear through the storm. They had been captives of *Grampa Woo* for almost 12 hours.

Grampa Woo II, the once sleek cruise ship owned by Captain Dana Kollars.

The minuscule *Westfort* continued to sink out of sight in bungalow-size waves. Disregarding an earlier directive that icing conditions made the vessel unsafe, it manoeuvred itself around and around, treading water, so to speak, continuously turning into the waves in order to maintain its position.

"Every wave that towered over us threatened to fling us broadside into a deadly roll."[14]

Although given the option to leave by the Rescue Coordination Centre (RCC) in Trenton, Ontario, the crew of the *Westfort* felt duty bound, despite their own peril, to stay to assist the *Glenada* should anyone go overboard or a ship swamp.

"RCC comes on the phone and says you are no longer responsible if you leave, in other words, you can choose to leave, that's your decision. We looked at each other and I said: 'Well?' They wanted to stay. They didn't want to leave. They knew damn well, they could lose their lives. But they wanted to stay. So, I felt I was with the right bunch."[15]

Meanwhile, the once sleek tour boat was transforming into a grizzled and unsteady derelict.

"Wallowing in the trough, wallowing back and forth and they were rolling to the point that they were starting to worry whether they were going to go right over."[16]

Grampa Woo was no longer a cruise ship of opulent tranquility. No longer obedient and compliant at the end of the *McCarthy*'s towline, it was completely out-of-control. It had become some sort of creature, rolling longways in the waves and flinging its former masters from side to side, sometimes smashing them against the unrelenting wall of the bulkhead, never allowing them to rest. With the battering came mental anguish. How long could they survive? Would the ship roll right over and drown them? Would they be carried down the shipping channel and out to sea? Would this formerly proud ship self-destruct somewhere on the islands of the sprawling archipelago of Isle Royale or farther out on the rocky shore of Lake Superior, oblivious to the fate of the men inside?

Everyone knew it was unlikely the two men would survive if not rescued. Desperation had driven them to consider getting into one of the mesh-bottomed life rafts stored onboard for the passengers. They were wearing only life jackets and wet suits, one just the top.

"Getting into that Lake, that was the scariest prospect."[17]

"I would have even stayed with the boat onto the rocks first."[18]

Even though the *Glenada* had turned back towards them, how was it going to get the men off the *Grampa Woo*? The problem of trying to throw frozen heaving lines from frozen gloves still existed. The wind, snow and black, the perpetual rising and falling of the waves, continued to intensify. The *Glenada* Captain knew the men could not survive in the mesh-bottom life rafts. Could the *Westfort* rescue the men? "No" came the answer. A helicopter had been ordered by the *Westfort* Coxswain, but would the men last the hours it would take for the helicopter to arrive, if, with the storm, it could arrive? Would it be able to retrieve the men from a bouncing deck or life raft? The Captain shouted a daring plan to his crewman. The crewman agreed. It was their last chance. The hour that seemed like days had exhausted all plans, except one.

On shore, Sharon Dawson, wife of the *Glenada's* Captain, monitored not only her three children, Nathan, Heather, and Davis, but the terse exchanges on the radio channels

Coxswain Ed Greer watches Lake Superior from Hillcrest Park in Thunder Bay, the way he watched it *that night* when his wife, Inga Thorsteinson, was participating in the rescue from *Grampa Woo*.

in the home office of the family businesses, Thunder Bay Tug Services and Thunder Bay Marine Services. She was concerned but basically confident in her man, his ship and its crew. Her mother-in-law, the Captain's mother, Wealthy Dawson, escaped worry because she was not told. Some hundred and thirty miles away in Beaver Bay, Minnesota, ChunAe (pronounced Chn-Aye) Kollars, wife of *Grampa Woo*'s Captain, phoned Sharon Dawson for information and consolation. Ed Greer, the husband of one of the crew on the *Westfort*—himself the Coxswain of the other crew—sat staring into the dark of the park, identifying with her danger and knowing that sitting there was really all he could do. Francis Moore, the mother of Barb Maki, girlfriend of one of the crewmen on the *Westfort*, went to the Coast Guard station to get Fritz, his German Shepherd, which had been left at the base. The Chief Coxswain's girlfriend, Magdelena Mann, waited, his dog safely at home.

Gerry Dawson, the Captain of the tug *Glenada*.

Joyce Olson, wife of the engineer on the *Glenada*, bustled about her handcraft store to keep busy, realizing the dangers, but, like Sharon Dawson, confident of her man, the ship and its crew. Meghan Balmer, wife of the crewman careening about the icy deck of the *Glenada*, was blissfully ignorant of how bad it was. The city of Thunder Bay tensed itself for the news. It was tense for three days.

Lake Superior was a major participant in the drama by simply being there. In its own way, it was reacting to the down drafts and air currents racing along both sides of the long body of the Sleeping Giant peninsula towards Thunder Cape and to the funnel of north-west wind pouring across Thunder Bay into the open sea of Lake Superior.

Struggling out on the water were: Captain Gerry (pronounced Garry) Dawson, crewman Jim Harding and engineer Jack Olson on the *Glenada*; Chief Coxswain Bob King and crew Inga Thorsteinson and Willie Trognitz on the

Westfort; Captain Dana Kollars and crewman Robin Sivill on the *Grampa Woo*; Captain Lawrence (Larry) Smyth and crew on the *Walter J. McCarthy Jr.*

From these names, one would emerge as a hero, a hero amongst heroes. It was Gerry Dawson.

2 ~ THE EIGHTH SEA

Each blade of grass has its spot on earth whence it draws its life, its strength.

Around its almost 1,826 miles[1] of shore is a small, like-minded body of devotees who rarely know each other. They are devoted, in an almost religious way, to Lake Superior.

"To me, it's like a mirror held to God."[2]

These devotees steward the Lake, play in it, study it, and in a mystical, non-linguistic way, feel they communicate through it with the universe of which they are a part. Somehow they feel they understand—perhaps experience—their place in the spectrum of existence; the meaning, some would say, of spirituality. Because this communication is individual and direct, their need for human validation is unnecessary. The need for words is unnecessary. Their experience with the Lake is immediate, consuming, and virtually inexpressible. They seek and find their solitary joy alone.

For some of those with the love, and it is love, the draw of the sea—Lake Superior is an inland sea, the largest surface of fresh water in the world—it would seem there is almost a *species memory* when the evolving human was, perhaps, an *aquatic ape*. Seemingly, it lived out the heat of the Pliocene Age, which lasted some ten or twelve million years, partly submerged in water. There, the human learned to stand upright, shed most of its body hair, developed subcutaneous fat and a very human nose, and found solace and protection in the sea from the heat and predators on land. Some seem not to have forgotten those ancient days.[3]

Gerry Dawson felt that sense of home on, by, and in the water.

"Lake Superior has been in my blood ever since I was born. It seems it's always been like a drawing card or a magnet. It's always pulling me back to the Lake. I could never live without the water."[4]

Gerry Dawson may have developed this feeling from his parents who made their living on the Lake. As long as he can remember, he worked and played in and around the fjords and inlets of its lengthy northwestern Ontario coastline. Lake Superior also touches Minnesota, Wisconsin, and Michigan. But, where did his parents get the drive to be on water? There are no mariners in their ancestry, except a great uncle in the navy. Gerry's mother, Wealthy Dawson, always felt the lure of water and, as a girl, frolicked on and in Lake Ontario. As far as anyone knows, her

The water of life.

husband, Elliott, had no ancestors on the water, but he nevertheless chose the life of the sea.

Another devotee, Captain Dana Kollars of Lake Superior Excursions and owner of the *Grampa Woo*, came from a farm in Nebraska. His father was afraid of water. Yet Dana seemed born to love it and believes it may be from his Norwegian heritage.

"By the time I was in the fifth grade building my own small skiff, I've always been on the water."[5]

Captains Dawson and Kollars also belong to another group. They are users. They work on and with the Lake. Unlike devotees, users are very much aware of each other and belong to a loose, rather judgemental network of individuals who utilize the Lake as all or part of their livelihood.

"I knew everybody on the Lakes at one time."[6]

Users are part of the industry of the Lake. From the early fur-trading days and the voyageur canoes, to the freighters, ocean vessels, and tugs, shipping cargo on the Lake has increased explosively. In addition to the commercial operation, there is stowaway cargo. Ocean vessels transport hidden exotic species from other lands in their ballast water which is pumped out into Lake Superior harbours before the ship is loaded. Zebra mussels, ruffe, round goby, and carp have all found homes here, with varying effects on their new environment.[7] Recommendations for voluntary exchange of salt water ballast for fresh water from the mouth of the St. Lawrence is the beginning of a solution.

Industries reliant on water transportation, such as grain elevators, pulp and paper, mining, and wood preservers, cluster along the shore of Lake Superior's towns and cities. Both anglers and commercial fisheries delight in the relatively untainted salmon, trout, whitefish and herring, although there are fish advisories against many species and sizes.[8] Cruise ships show off Lake Superior's beauty.

As a part of the developing tourism industry, Dana Kollars is concerned about the loss of natural waterfront resulting from unrestricted building and thoughtless clearing. He calls the view of the land from the water the "viewshed." He is also concerned about pollution.

> "I know in the bottom of my heart the things that are most important to be done aren't going to be done."[9]

Similarly, Gerry Dawson is concerned. He remembers when he was younger actually seeing raw sewage floating around his tugs.[10]

For years some of the users have regarded the Lake as a garbage dump: the city of Thunder Bay using it somewhat like a sewer; Northern Wood Preservers in Thunder Bay using it as a repository for the seepage and spills from its treatment plant. "The contaminants which are generally associated with the NWP facility include oil and grease, chlorophenols, polychlorinated biphenyls, PAHs, dioxins, furans, and the metals As, Cu and Cr (arsenic, copper chromium). Cadmium, lead and mercury have also been found at elevated concentrations in the harbour sediments; however, no clear source for these metals has been determined at present."[11] The U.S. Army Corps of Engineers allowed at least 1437 barrels of waste, some containing barium, lead, benzene, cadmium and PCB's, to be dumped north of Duluth/Superior around mid-century.[12]

> "I consider it my Lake or part of my Lake, and to have people contaminating it or polluting it, it's...I feel badly about it."[13]

Although feeling badly is the first step towards solution, government-appointed Public Advisory Committees (PAC) to the Remedial Action Plans (RAP) for the Great Lakes do more. All PAC members have varying stakes in the proceedings, some representing industry, some representing various community organizations, some with purely altruistic motivation. The committed members recognize the importance of environmental health, and the need not only to remediate past problems but to create a climate of respect for water habitat of all creatures. These volunteer committees are a break-through in both provincial and federal government recognition of the importance of public participation in policy-making. Advising the Remedial Action Plan team—paid government employees—on the importance of the problems set before them, these committees are not costly. On the north shore of Lake Superior, the five PAC RAPs, as they are called, have a ratio of 46 volunteer members to six staff.[14]

Both Dana and Gerry are pleased there is a growing interest in the environment. Yet, what is not raising concern is the airborne deposition of chemicals from inside and outside the Lake Superior basin.

> "More than 95 percent of the persistent toxic organic substances entering Lake Superior comes through the air, the remainder comes from effluent pipes or run-off."[15]

The contaminants cannot help but affect the fish, even in its deepest waters. The effect on humans of breathing bad air and ingesting tainted fish is only beginning to be documented. The health survey project, *Effects on Aboriginals from the Great Lakes Environment (EAGLE)*, suggests that "First Nations people from the Lake Superior region are less healthy than those of other regions."[16] It found that Lake Superior aboriginals eat more fish and game than those in any other Great Lakes area. A correlation between these two findings has yet to be established.

Some harbourfronts in urban areas are off limits because of industry. Toxic water laps the shore. Years of thoughtless use deposited not only chemicals but debris. Concentrated efforts by the PAC RAPs, Great Lakes Programs and Sea Grants have led to the removal of much of this debris. These advocates also want the water detoxified to acceptable standards.

Eight sites on Lake Superior have been designated 'Areas of Concern' or 'hot spots' by the International Joint Commission, the St. Mary's River at the easterly end counting as part of Lake Superior. In all, there are presently 42 hot spots on the Great Lakes.[17]

The despoilers and the devotees are rarely one and the same. Occasionally, a user is a devotee. Such is Captain Dawson.

"What's my favourite kind of work on Superior? Anything."[18]

Such is Captain Kollars.

"It didn't take me long to realize that taking people charter fishing on Lake Superior not only involved the act of catching fish, but it also involved a service whereby people could be introduced to these fantastically wonderful resources, both natural and cultural."[19]

Dana might be called a bigamist because of his attitude to Lake Superior.

"I prefer to call Lake Superior my second wife. There are times if you're married that your voyage isn't always nice. There are times when you're sailing that you have conflicts. There are times when she's going to be placid and pleasant and beautiful again. Its vastness...to see the moon and the reflection on the water...you can look at what we call the stairway to heaven, yes, yes, a definite love."[20]

Dana's first wife is a petite, wasp-waisted Korean bride of 25 years whose name ChunAe means 'spring love.' She is office manager and receptionist for their business. The screen saver logo on the computer reads, 'ChunAe, I wuv woo.'

Many who use the Lake and survive, right from the easterly end at Sault Ste. Marie, such as Captain Frank Prouse, to the westerly end at Thunder Bay, such as Captain Dawson, use one word to describe their attitude in dealing with Lake Superior: respect. If the word 'respect' is not in the vocabulary of anyone on or near the Lake, trouble may result.

"You learn to respect the Lake. Every so many years, you get a lesson out there and it reminds you of who's boss. I've seen it go from flat calm and foggy up to fifteen foot waves in a matter of one and-a-half to two hours."[21]

Often, if someone, out of ignorance or forgetfulness or heedlessness, ventures beyond their capabilities, the Lake rarely overlooks it. There is little margin for error. Ships sink or are blown on rocks. Snowmobilers drop through the ice, dwellings built too close to the water are undercut by waves, and docks rarely survive.

"I've got a lot of respect. Never take anything for granted out there. Too much can happen too fast. The Lake can blow up so quick. I've seen it. I've been out there just for pleasure, just fishing off the end of Isle Royale and you can see it coming, and all of a sudden, there's thunder storms and thirty knot winds out of nowhere. You have to go hide fast. It's tricky. It's no place to fool around. Anybody who doesn't know what they're doing, shouldn't be out there. I see these people running around in small boats and things like that; some of them take awful chances. They're relying on the weather they get off the radio—and it's not always going to happen that way, or when. Sometimes, I've only got fifty miles from town and had to go and hide for a couple of days."[22]

Early mythology of the Greeks predicts that disdain and disrespect towards forces greater than the human will be punished. In the theory of J.E. Lovelock, the Earth and all its components are a living creature, one organism.[23] If this hypothesis is carried a logical step further, it would follow that as certain activities begin to threaten the organism which is planet Earth, the purveyors of those activities will be expunged, just as a functioning immune system will expunge a threatening pathogen, just as an arrogant sailor will be forced to come to terms with unrecognized weakness, just as prideful Greeks were punished by the gods. Both Lake Superior and the Earth are like haughty Greek goddesses, Lake Superior expunging the disrespectful, so too perhaps the Earth.

Lake Superior preens herself in splendour 600 feet above the ocean's surface and 731 feet below it. Its beauty and benevolence, its often placid comeliness, are misleading.

"You never know what's going to come and it happens so fast. It changes so quickly. Even the pilots that come up here, that's what they say. They say, 'If you don't like the weather, wait for ten minutes, it's going to change.'"[24]

Lake Superior looks like a sea deity. Its mesas and cuestas, crags and cliffs, its mountainous sand dunes, protrude like the merlons of a giant's crown 1,000 feet above its sapphire depths.

"Those who have never seen Superior get an inadequate, even inaccurate idea, by hearing it spoken of as a 'lake,' and to those who have sailed over its vast extent the word sounds positively ludicrous. Though its waters are fresh and crystal, Superior is a sea."[25]

Cradled by some of the oldest rock in the world from the tumultuously volcanic Precambrian era some three billion years ago,[26] sloshed for a time by the inland seas and sediments of the Paleozoic era beginning some 600 million years ago, Lake Superior's rocks were then swept, excoriated, and compressed, by the gigantic glaciers of the Pleistocene epoch beginning more than a million years ago.

The lavas and granites, sediments and intrusions accumulated during more than five-sixths of Earth's existence so far[27] were weathered and scoured by the lumbering glaciers. Lakes, cliffs, and depressions caused by the weight of the glaciers were re-arranged. Towering rock shapes remained. Water levels in what would be the Lake Superior basin were adjusted producing a succession of terraces, abandoned beaches and abrupt escarpments.[28] Some say the effects of the last glacier, finally receding some 11,500 years ago,[29] are still being felt, the north shore of Lake Superior apparently still springing up some 18 inches a century.[30]

So far, Lake Superior's existence has been a three-act drama: the first volcanic; the second sea action, sediments, and early life; and the third glacial, either still continuing or moving into act four. No-one really knows. Contrary to perception, geology is never static.

Voices from as early as 9,000 years ago echo across the recently-shaped land at the northwestern end of the Lake.[31] Evidence of the earliest human occupation of Lake Superior comes from the Paleo-Indian sites at Pass Lake in the vicinity of Thunder Bay.[32] Legends of the early people still whisper in the imagination. Nanabijou, Gitche-Gumee, Mishipishiw and Windigo are alive in the rocks and waters.

Into the vast expanses of water and land with its sparse indigenous populations came the explorers, the missionaries, the fur traders and the settlers. French explorers initially labelled Lake Superior, 'supérieur' because it was uppermost of the five Great Lakes. On Coronelli's 1688 map of western New France, it was called Lac de Tracy,[33] named after Lieutenant General Alexandre de Prouville de

Tracy of New France who died in 1670. Glacial Lake Duluth is the name given to the early glacial meltwater that ponded in the south-west quarter during Lake Superior's formation.[34] Many believe its present name, Superior, aptly implies 'best.'

Beautiful and demanding, icily transparent, Lake Superior is clear, cold, and still relatively clean, despite defilement by those oblivious to its meaning.

Most striking is Lake Superior's clarity. Shimmering below the surface, glacial boulders can be seen more than 40 feet down.[35] It is not unusual to see red igneous rock stripped with white sand some 100 feet out. Lake Superior's bays, river mouths and southern shores are less clear. For instance, the visibility in Nipigon Bay is ten feet or less.[36]

Lake Superior is the least far along of the Great Lakes in the eutrophication process. While the production and decay of plants and organisms are sometimes natural, they mostly result from pollutants such as phosphates and fertilizers. With few nutrient loadings relative to its size entering the Lake, there is little to foster significant algae bloom and organism increase. Visibility averages 27 feet.[37] The dissolved oxygen content remains high because it is not being depleted by decomposing organics. Consequently, its ecological definition remains oligotrophic, a definition originally applicable to all the Great Lakes.[38]

Contaminants in an oligotrophic lake, having little to which they can attach, stay in suspension for longer. A drop of water remains in Lake Superior for 191 years. Lake Erie's retention time is 2.6 years.[39]

Clear. Also cold. The coldest of the Great Lakes.

"The mean depth of Superior is 489 feet and temperatures at that depth remain relatively constant and near 39.2 Fahrenheit."[40]

Although the mean annual temperature is 38.5 Fahrenheit, the surface waters of the Lake are coldest in

February to early April, about 32 degrees Fahrenheit, and warmest in early September, 61 Fahrenheit.[41] In summer the lake is quite swimmable with temperatures higher than 70 degrees Fahrenheit recorded near shore.

On *that night* of October 30, 1996, the mean surface temperature off-shore from Thunder Cape likely would have been about 44 Fahrenheit.[42] By comparison, the temperature of the average refrigerator ranges from 40 to 44 degrees Fahrenheit.

"You would live for about 30 minutes before the cold sucked the life out of you."[43]

Clear. Cold. Also clean, relatively speaking. It is the cleanest of the Great Lakes.

At the approach of the millennium, the appearance of dealing with Lake Superior's despoilage is greater than its actuality. Governments, strapped by earlier spendthrift and debt-developing ways, struggled with constructing an appearance of management, an appearance that often did not coincide with reality. These appearances were accepted because human life had not been sufficiently impaired to cause alarm in the general population.

A change in attitude appeared to begin. In varying degrees, Sault Ste. Marie and Duluth created aesthetic, accessible and workable waterfronts. The city of Thunder Bay planned—and planned—to build a secondary treatment plant for its sewage, and to make its waterfront not only available to the people but environmentally healthy. The water near all three cities had been designated a 'hot spot' of pollution.

Because of intense pressure by some citizenry and the Thunder Bay PAC RAP, Northern Wood Preservers joined forces with the two other companies associated with the site, Canadian National Railway and Abitibi Pulp and Paper. They proposed a plan to the federal and provincial governments to initiate voluntary containment and treatment of part of the 'blob,' eight football fields of creosote and contaminated soil and sediments on the harbourfront. Ventures such as these appeared to be a beginning.

> "I don't like to see anyone polluting the Lake. I have to make a living off it and I like to drink the water out of it—it's the cleanest water you can get—and to have someone polluting it..."[44]

Acts of polluting seem insignificant because of Lake Superior's size. With 31,700 square miles,[45] the jagged crescent of Lake Superior is the largest lake in the world by surface area, the second largest by volume, surpassed only by mile-deep Lake Baikal in Siberia.[46] With its shoreline stretching 1,826 miles, it equals almost the distance from Thunder Bay to Halifax. It is 350 miles long and 160 miles wide.

The deepest of the Great Lakes, Lake Superior's shoreline drops off quickly and sharply to an average depth of 489 feet. Along the western shore, the Lake drops to 700 feet within less than three miles of shore. Its deepest depression is 1,333 feet near Munising, Michigan,[47] capable of drowning all but the TV mast of the Empire State Building.

The Lake contains three quadrillion gallons of water, half of the water in the Great Lakes. Spread out, the water of Lake Superior could flood Canada, the U.S., Mexico and South America with one foot of water.[48] No doubt its reservoir of ten percent of the world's fresh surface water[49] is being eyed covetously by economic developers, politicians, and those in need of water either because of despoilage or over-population.

Despite its size, Lake Superior does not have tides. However, because of its ebullient storms, the piling up of water in part of the Lake, known as a 'wind tide' or 'wind set-up,' often accompanied by dramatic atmospheric changes, pulls the water away from distant shores, producing an oscillation called a 'seiche' (pronounced saysh). The slow motion, sloshing effect, like a wave in a bathtub, can continue long after its cause has passed. Rarely is the lake level affected more than about one foot. However, in July, 1995, at the Eastern end of the lake, the water was pulled out more than 100 feet.

"Eventually the water went right out past the end of my dock [near the St. Mary's River] and I have over 100 feet of dock. It was fascinating because children were out playing in the sand, everybody's boat was on the ground, tilted over. I have an ATV [All Terrain Vehicle] and I got on that and rode all around the shore, way up about a mile, way out in the water which would have been around my neck. Shipping was halted on the river because the boats were

Lake Superior seiche.

drawing too much water. They couldn't navigate because the water had dropped so much they were dragging on the bottom. Some of them couldn't get over the sill at the locks on the St. Mary's River and they had to wait until the water came back."[50]

Just past Whitefish Bay, also at the eastern end of the Lake, sound was added to the visual phenomenon.

"A rumbling, progressively louder, as of a low-flying airplane, approached from the west, sounding like a subway train underground. Maybe five minutes later, the rumbling came again. This time, I went outside and looked at the shore. 'The tide' had gone out as if in the Atlantic Ocean."[51]

It took from one to five hours for the water to return to normal levels. "Very slowly, it crept back."[52] Although dramatic seiches like this are rare, there are usually one or two a year on Lake Superior.[53]

"Seiches, though rare, are well understood on the Great Lakes as a result of a unique set of weather condition and geography, and can indeed be deadly enough to sink a boat or small ship."[54]

There are other strange effects on Lake Superior. On occasion, the water and the sky will form an eerie, continuous dome with no horizon; rocks, islands and ships appear to be floating in the air. Sun dogs glisten in the sky as the sun's rays bounce along the clouds and northern lights flap like sheets on the sky's invisible clothes line. At sunset, there can be the most evanescent, magical light and rocks glow an iridescent orange.

As in the Arctic, there can be strange mirages. Quite regularly, the enormous rock toe and foot of the Sleeping Giant at the foot of the Sibley Peninsula seems to protrude from the water, the horizon line somewhere around its

The toe of the Sleeping Giant is in the air.

ankles. Tall buildings can appear on the horizon where there are no tall buildings. Mountainous terrain can appear where there is no land, even for a hundred or more miles.

In winter, the mixture of churning water and freezing temperatures sculpt Henry Moore icebergs, caves and stalactites, which often turn a translucent turquoise as the winter season progresses. The ice booms as it freezes up, causing dogs to bark at the unusual sound. Often the ice reverberates with a long, hollow wail as if Orpheus were blowing across the neck of a bottle. The sound of chattering birds are really the voices of ice fragments jostling each other, and conversations of people in a deserted bay are found to be the conversations of ice.

Storms, although rare, are beautiful and intimidating in their power. However, much of the time Lake Superior is a serene, calm goddess, lapping and gurgling in peaceful pleasure around its multi-facetted shore.

Of course, Lake Superior does not gurgle in pleasure. It is not a haughty or serene goddess. Its storms are not, literally speaking, horrific, its waves angry or mean. The sea is not cruel. These kinds of words simply reflect the human describing the world in terms of itself, the adjectives unconsciously revealing an attitude; human fears and needs being projected onto something else, often an attempt to make the human appear superior. Dominance or humility? Arrogance or respect? These are the essential questions of survival both on the Lake and in the world. The rather boastful slogan of the Remedial Action Plan for Lake Superior, *Making a Great Lake Superior*, certainly would cause a rumble of displeasure in the early Greek god of the sea, Poseidon, or the haughty goddess of Superior, if either existed. Gaia, if she exists, would happily take RAP's help, boastful or not.

Respect for Lake Superior was crucial the night before Halloween, October 30, 1996. It played a part in the survival of eight people. That night would forever remain in Gerry Dawson's mind as "that night."[55]

The storm began gathering strength the night before. After attending a meeting, Gerry Dawson, alerted by his wife Sharon, drove to the dock by the old Thunder Bay Elevator and Saskatchewan Wheat Pool 7A where his tugs were moored. He and his partner, Rolland (Rollie) Frayne, who lives on the tug, the *Point Valour*—"He says he's going to die there"[56]—stood watching and worrying as the fenders of the *Point Valour* and the *Glenada* rammed against the dock.

"At approximately 10 p.m., the wind was howling out of the east at 35-40 knots. The seas were running four to six feet in the elevator slips and testing the strength of the mooring with every wave."[57]

The men quickly realized the tugs had to be moved to a safer mooring at Pool 8 on the Kaministiquia River. Gerry rushed home and changed his clothes. The crews of both ships were called out. By early morning, although the wind slightly subsided, it had ominously backed around to the north-west, a counter-clockwise wind shift usually predicating bad weather. The tugs received a call to help move the *John J. Boland*. They would help it navigate up river to the Avenor Mill. By the time they reached their destination, the storm had more than regained its strength from the night before.

"The wind was 40-45 knots and was picking the top off the water and creating waterspouts. And this was in a sheltered river."[58]

In the minds of those who know the Lake, and especially in the minds of those intimately affected, this storm will be remembered as "the *Grampa Woo* storm."

"All shipping on the Lake had stalled, with 18 ships at anchor in Whitefish Bay, and 8 to 10 in Thunder Bay."[59]

A tour is being conducted for the Public Advisory Committee aboard the *Glenada* to see the beginning of the Northern Woods Preservers' clean-up. The ship, at right, contains the worst of the dredged contaminants.

The storm of November 10, 1975, is remembered as "the *Fitzgerald* storm" because it sank the *Edmund Fitzgerald* with all hands. It was the flag ship of the fleet, the Titanic of the Great Lakes. Twenty-nine men were lost. There were no survivors. Only a fictional one in a later novel.[60] This storm fostered greater humility in Lake Superior mariners. Equipment was improved, and ships sought out shelter in storms, no longer regarding themselves as invincible.

The storm of November 18, 1985, is remembered as "the *Socrates* storm" because it blew this moored Liberian saltie hard aground at Duluth, a foreshadowing of *Grampa Woo*. The year 1905 is remembered because multiple storms claimed 78 lives, culminating in the November 28 storm which involved 30 vessels in marine casualties.[61]

Over 350 vessels have been lost in Lake Superior and over a thousand incidents have been investigated. More than one thousand people have lost their lives in shipwrecks.[62]

Tugs pull the *Socrates* off the beach at Duluth after a storm blew its mooring.

What exactly is a storm? A storm has a specific definition in terms of wind force and sea criteria. Contrary to popular thinking, a storm is stronger than a gale or strong gale. In fact, a violent storm is next to the hurricane in force. On Lake Superior, it is not the gales of November which cause the problems. It is the storms of November, actually the storms of autumn. And the hurricanes force winds.

> "Usually around the solstice season and the equinox, you get a blow. Within a week either side of them, you usually get a pretty good blow."[63]

The assessment of storms and gales was objectively categorized almost two centuries ago.

> "A scale of wind velocity was devised (c. 1805) by Admiral Sir Francis Beaufort of the British navy."[64]

Adaptations of Beaufort's scale are used both by the U.S. Weather Bureau and the Canadian Coast Guard. The force of the wind is rated on a scale using numbers from zero to 12. Zero represents *calm*; one represents *light air*; two *light breeze*; three *gentle breeze*; four *moderate breeze*; five *fresh breeze*; six *strong breeze*; seven *near gale*; eight *gale*; nine *strong gale*; ten *storm*; eleven *violent storm*; twelve *hurricane*. Wind velocity is usually measured on an anemometer, an instrument which catches and measures the wind as it revolves around a central rod.

Wind velocity also can be categorized by sea criteria agreed upon by the International Meteorological Committee in 1939. Neither the *Glenada* nor the *Westfort* had an anemometer and used sea criteria and experience to gauge wind speed.

With *gale* force winds, the waves are ruffled with white crests and the likely prototype of the sea creature of Ojibwa lore, the great sea lynx, Mishipishiw, begins to rise from the depths, mane flying as it submerges into the waves. As the winds increase, Mishipishiw appears again, bigger, bolder, power bars radiating from its crest, flinging foam along the length of the wave.

A *storm* has winds up to 48 to 55 knots or up to 63 miles per hour. It has the following sea criteria.

"Very high waves with long overhanging crests. The resulting foam, in great patches, is blown in dense white streaks along the direction of the wind. On the whole, the surface of the sea takes on a white appearance. The tumbling of the sea becomes heavy and shock-like. Visibility is affected."[65]

A *violent storm* has winds from 56 to 63 knots or up to 72 miles per hour and has the following sea criteria.

"Exceptionally high waves. (Small and medium sized ships might be for a time lost to view behind the waves.) The sea is completely covered with long white patches of foam lying along the direction of the wind. Everywhere the edges of the wave crests are blown into froth. Visibility affected."[66]

With a *hurricane*, the wind speed is 64 knots, 73 miles per hour, and over.

"The air is filled with foam and spray. Sea completely white with driving spray. Visibility very seriously affected."[67]

On the eve of October 30, 1996, Chief Coxswain Bob King of the Canadian Coast Guard Cutter *Westfort* called the winds "11 force," which would be a *violent storm.* Captain Dawson called them "storm force winds," although he later said the winds were "70 knots." Captain Kollars said the National Weather Service reported the barometric pressure was equivalent to that of the eye of a hurricane in Minnesota. Captain Smyth of the *McCarthy* said the winds were reading "over 60 knots"[68] on the anemometer.

At Trowbridge Island near Thunder Cape, two and-a-half miles from the struggling ships and at the north portal of the bay of Thunder Bay, an automated Environment Canada weather station documented the winds varying from *hurricane* force in late morning to *violent storm* when the ships turned towards Thunder Bay.

The assessments of the experienced captains involved were unanimous in their opinion there were storm force winds, maybe violent storm force winds, maybe even hurricane force. It is a tribute to the understatement of the captains that the United States Coast Guard Marine Casualty Report officially lists the winds at 70 knots, hurricane force.[69]

The Environment Canada weather station may have recorded less intense winds at the time of the rescue, either because its hourly records missed the hurricane gusts[70] or because there may have been a microclimate by Trowbridge Island. It is not unusual to stand near wavy, even calm water and see the jagged peaks of huge waves out on the horizon.

Obviously, though, it is not just the storms that cause problems. It is the Lake's reaction to the storm. Waves result from the combined effect of the force of the wind along with how long it blows and how far it travels over the water. "Speed, duration and fetch."[71]

Waves begin with what is called a 'cat's paw,' the wind just touching the water and brushing a thousand diamond shapes into the imprint. These tiny shapes are called *capillary waves*. The wind is scratching the lake in order to get traction to create full-blown waves, which happen at about six knots.[72]

In mid-ocean where the water is cold and deep, the waves may be big, but they are regular and predictable.

"That's the trouble with Lake Superior. We are getting deflections from Sibley Peninsula and we're getting it off Pie Island and I don't know if I could say

The beginning of wind.

we were getting it all the way from Isle Royale but all these different wave patterns converge. Three different wave patterns."[73]

Waves can overtake each other and form groups creating a burgeoning wave pattern that climaxes into a crescending peak or episodic wave.

"Reports by ship crews are very rare; if a ship happens to experience a huge episodic wave, it very likely sinks without a trace because of its tremendous destructive power."[74]

Such a wave pattern could account for the 15 or so vessels that have 'went missing' without a trace on Lake Superior[75] and why the *Edmund Fitzgerald* never transmitted the universally recognized distress call "M'aidez"—now Mayday—once "Venez m'aidez"[76]—before it sank.

On Lake Superior, there is a phenomenon called "the three sisters"—some say "the seven sisters"[77]—an ascending wave grouping that luxuriates in a final powerful episodic wave that can curl into a towering cascade of platinum foam, beautiful to admirers, deadly to the unaware. Some say it is a wall of solid water with only trickles of overflow down its vertical face. Few survive to say.

Captain Gerry Dawson tells of another wave phenomenon *that night* of October 30.

> "We had wind coming out of Thunder Bay and it was also coming out of the southwest up from the other side of Pie Island. What was happening was the waves and the wind coming together pretty well right at Thunder Cape, creating what they call a cross-sea, where two seas go in different directions. They call it 'haystacking' when the waves crash together."[78]

Even the ordinary, every day kind of waves on Lake Superior and the Great Lakes are thought to be unique.

> "A big difference from the ocean. The seas in the ocean are long—long and not all that steep—whereas, here on the Lakes, they are short, fast and really ugly. They come at you fast and they're steep. The fresh water's a lot lighter than the salt water. It gets going faster. Things calm down faster afterwards, too, but when something comes up like a storm or even a gale comes up, it pushes that water in a big hurry. A 60 foot sea out on the ocean is just like a big roller coaster ride. You get something half that size here and you're just dancing."[79]

On the other hand, there is a peaceful pattern of wave groupings that happens even in storms. Mariners call it a 'window.' A window is basically a lull or a flat spot. Any beach walker knows how the waves can retreat by ten or fifteen feet, giving a person a chance to, say, quickly cross a surge-filled cove. Back come the waves though, reaching up and up grabbing at the ankles or sometimes worse, sweeping the unwary off their feet.

On *that night* of October 30, 1996, the *Westfort* delegated one person to spot not only the direction of oncoming waves from the back of the ship, necessary because the windshield was iced up, but to watch for the windows too. A window may have even provided a special opportunity which Captain Dawson of the *Glenada* had the capability of seizing as elusive *Grampa Woo* continually defied being captured and brought in tow again.

3 ~ THE WOMEN IN HIS LIFE

The marital relations of seamen would make an interesting subject, and I could tell you instances …

The night he was named Harbour Man of the Year, February 28, 1997—which some say he deserved years ago—Captain Dawson thanked two of the three women in his life.

"I would like to thank my wife, Sharon, who is my anchor and steadying force."[1]

On the chain around Sharon's neck, the letters *SISU* have been cast in solid gold. Because she is Finnish, she has known all her life that *SISU* meant "guts." She cherishes the necklace, not because her life had been unduly tough, not in terms of what women have to deal with in many parts of the world, but she cherishes the necklace because of what it exemplifies. The Finnish people, especially her grandmother, born Aili Olga Hanni, possess a clear-eyed recognition of the fact that all life is tough; it takes guts to deal with life; yet it can be good. Grandmother Aili, born to a first generation homesteading family in Whitewood, Saskatchewan, became a teacher, married twice, and had 13 children.

"I remember her always busy, always helping others."[2]

Sharon's mother, Doris Laine (from Linjatie) Arnold, had two family rings melted down. From the gold she had *SISU* necklaces made for her sisters, for Sharon and for herself, in memory of her mother's joyfulness in dealing with a difficult life. Sharon's life has not been particularly easy. Sharon's mother-in-law, Wealthy Goodman Dawson, understood. She too could be wearing a necklace with *SISU* on it. To her, Gerry Dawson is grateful.

Sharon Dawson, Gerry's wife, his support and the companies' business manager.

"I would like to thank my mother...[she] being the calming influence in my life."[3]

In 1952, after ten years of marriage and a life in southern Ontario, Wealthy and her husband, Elliott, set off from Niagara-on-the-Lake for Port Arthur, now the city of Thunder Bay. They had to navigate from Lake Ontario, through lakes Erie and Huron, to their destination on the most western shore of the uppermost lake, Lake Superior, some 1,000 miles (800 nautical miles) away. Sailing on a 36 foot, gasoline-powered, air-force crash boat purchased in Toronto, they converted it into a Bum Boat or floating store. A tuck shop. It was called the *Joyell*.

"El got a job at the Port Weller Shipyard for a dollar an hour—he was a stationery engineer along with all his marine credentials—and so the Port Weller Shipyard allowed him to bring the boat into the dock there and then all the shipyard workers helped out after five o'clock. I built a clothes closet and did it with a template. The whole thing, nothing is square, and all those shipyard guys came down after it was finished and they couldn't believe it. My father was a carpenter by trade and I said I must have taken after him."[4]

Doing carpentry work and planning an adventurous thousand mile boat trip and a new life in Port Arthur was all taken in stride by Wealthy. She was unaware she was stepping into a mind-set, a way of life, entirely different from the peopled existence of urban southern Ontario. Some call it "the experience of North."[5] However, Wealthy regarded herself as "a real tomboy"[6] and understood water because she "was around the Bay of Quinte"[7] all her life. She and her cousin, Wallace, who was killed overseas during the war, had had many an adventure together on the water. Wealthy knew how to adjust.

Wealthy had grown up with her grandparents, her mother and sister, aunt, uncle, Wallace, and another cousin, in the grandparents' home in Point Anne, about seven miles from Belleville on Lake Ontario. Born in Brantford in 1924, her father died when she was a year and-a-half old, her mother only 29. Later, Wealthy would emulate the welcoming arms of her grandmother when she had her mother live with her for five years before her mother's death. It was in the port city of Point Anne, while Wealthy worked as a lab technician for 37 1/2 cents an hour at Canada Cement, that she met Elliott, who was an oiler on the *Cement Carrier*.

"I guess it was just meant to be."[8]

They were married a year and-a-half later when she was 21, and returned to live in Elliott's home town of Queenston followed by a brief period in Niagara-on-the-Lake. Elliott worked in a shipyard and Wealthy in a dry goods store; together they planned their adventure northwestward.

They created their Bum Boat. The *Joyell* would service ships waiting to take on grain in the booming twin transhipment port cities of Port Arthur and Fort William, popularly known as the Lakehead. (The cities were amalgamated and re-named Thunder Bay in 1970). When the Dawsons arrived in 1952, there were 25 or more operating terminals, 14 in Port Arthur.[9] The prosperity continued for 30 years. By 1982, the Lakehead was handling 60 percent of Canada's wheat exports, the number one port in Canada.[10] It peaked in 1983. The sailors were the Dawson's captive market. Because the grain ships were only 250 to 400 feet[11] in length, they did not take long to be loaded. Sailors did not have time to disembark and shop. The shop had to come to them. The Dawson's Bum Boat was that shop.

> "In the days when we first came here, there might be 12 or 15 boats out in anchor and we'd go out to the boats at anchor and we'd put the ladder up and all the sailors would come down and the boat was outfitted just like a store with a counter and pop cooler, magazines, and they would have standing orders every month for their tobacco. We had everything there, dress clothing, dress boots, shoes, whatever. We also had dry cleaning pick-up and drop off. We had a sub post office. We used to get souvenirs. Some fellows would say: 'My wife's anniversary is coming up,' or her birthday. 'Do you think you could pick something up uptown?' In those days, we had no vehicle. We just depended on a friend, Len Stewart. I don't think we could have survived without him."[12]

Two events which transpired prior to the Bum Boat expedition across the Great Lakes were portents of Wealthy's future life. On the day they began their journey, there was an eclipse of the sun. All the Lakers were tied up, but her "husband was kind of daring" and hardly had they started out but she landed on the floor, the ham she was cooking on the stove nestled beside her.[13] It was back to port for the Dawsons. When they started out again, their trip across the Great Lakes would take a month, not a week as planned.

"We started running into fog and high winds and then when we hit Lake Superior, I'm pumping gas for the engine into the engine gas tank and trying to keep the spout steady and I'm praying and praying. We had trouble all the way across Lake Superior. The spark plugs were completely burned out."[14]

"You see, we had two gasoline engines on the boat and we got a shot of diesel fuel in our gas at Detroit, the previous boat that they had fuelled was diesel fuel, so when it comes time for us to get our gas and when we started across Lake Superior from the Sault and it starts backfiring just like a car and I'm pumping gas out of the tank into the engine and so when we got close to Passage Island, the entrance to Thunder Bay harbour, my husband just said 'stand up on the top of the boat, get a white tea towel and signal the Coast Guard.' "[15]

"The Coast Guard towed us in. I cooked for eight Coast Guards, butter tarts, apple pie. They didn't want me to leave."[16]

Not only would her life be daring—with dirty fuel and Passage Island to play a part in her life again—but she and her husband seemed to know when to stop being daring. They survived working on Lake Superior.

In addition to the ham landing on top of her as a portent of the different kind of life ahead, Elliott's canniness in business and recognition of the need for a Bum Boat in the growing port of Port Arthur was another. From 1948 to 1950, he had sailed to Port Arthur on package freighters and immediately recognized the business opportunity which would utilize his particular skills. Elliott had been sailing the Great Lakes with the freighters, been around

Captain Elliott Dawson, Gerry Dawson's father, posing at the wheel of the *Inca*, a museum ship moored at Kingston, Ontario in 1985.

the world with the navy, and had his Marine One licence and his third-class stationery engineer papers. His uncle in the SeaBees, a casualty during the war, may have influenced his turning towards the water.

"After Grade 12, just to get away from the home environment, he went sailing and it just went from there."[17]

Life was not easy for Wealthy. They lived on the boat from May until September. They had arrived at the Lakehead with only $50, the cash depleted because of the length of their journey and their engine problems. Elliott's father stepped in and sent them $1,000. Both Wealthy and Elliott worked to turn that grubsteak into a viable business to offer to their boys.

"I was the deckhand and at first the sailors laughed at me when I couldn't get lines up to an empty ship but I conquered it and then I graduated. I could run the boat, start the boat and run it. Then I put my husband back to crew and I ran the boat. The other boat— the *Rosalee D* we bought in '56. It was a diesel and you had to go down below in the engine room to start it. I steered it, but I didn't try to start it. The more you know, the more you have to do."[18]

The more you know, the more you have to do. Classic Dawson humour. It germinated in Wealthy and bloomed in her son, Gerry. His sense of humour contributes to his affability and ability to get along with people, engendering passionate loyalty in employees.

Soon after arriving in Port Arthur, the babies started coming, five children in less than ten years.

"I was married ten years—didn't have any children—and came to Thunder Bay and got five children and ten grandchildren."[19]

She now has 14 grandchildren. After her fifth child, Wealthy had her tubes tied, a radical procedure in the mindset of the early Sixties. Her legs were such a mess from varicose veins that no less than five consulting doctors agreed to her operation.

"When the Seaway first opened, we were going nearly 24 hours a day. I'd sit with the phone on my shoulder and feeding the baby with this hand and writing the orders down... Everything we've got, we've earned, really earned." [20]

With the opening of the St. Lawrence Seaway in 1959, the complexion of shipping changed. Ships were longer, now up to 730 feet, and called seven-thirties. With the loading time longer, now allowing sailors time to shop on shore, Dawson Crew Supplies was disbanded. Sailors no longer needed the convenience of a floating store.

There was another need for the Dawsons to fill. Thunder Bay Marine Services Ltd. was created in 1960 to service the

Even at 3 1/2, Gerry Dawson wears the hat of captaincy.

Three captains in one family. Left to right, Captain Stan Dawson, Captain Elliott Dawson, Wealthy Dawson and Captain Gerry Dawson.

ocean freighters now coming into port. It provided pilot dispatching, linesmen, commercial diving, garbage disposal, and
tug services. Another boat, the *Coastal Cruiser*, was acquired.

In this unique existence, Wealthy developed a survival pattern. Try to be a good person, especially relating to the family. Keep busy. Don't complain. Speak up. Don't panic. Her
talk and her actions, her concerns, are full of family. She has
a strong sense of protectiveness. Gerry knows.

"My mother was a financial wizard, too. My brothers
and sister used to always bug me. I don't know if she
took me under her wing, but she always looked after me
when it came to money. Whenever I made money, she
took me down to the bank and had me deposit it."[21]

Wealthy has survived and done well in a tough world,
not by being a shy, retiring, dependant flower, but by
standing up for what she believed. The meaning of her
existence is important to her.

"I may not go to church every Sunday, but I practise
my faith. I would never see anyone in need and I try
to be kind and do things for people."[22]

If she had known about the events happening on the
Lake the night of October 30, she said she would have
prayed.

As the demands of the business and her family began to
wane, especially after her husband died, she plunged into
other activities.

"You name it and I have done it."[23]

All her life, she kept busy. She has raised five children,
been to Hawaii five times, loves her desserts which she
makes, knits, gardens, has been Worthy Matron of the
Eastern Star, does volunteer work for senior citizens and
reads, as well as looks after grandchildren.

Although not reluctant to speak her mind, she is not a

complainer. There is an underlying suggestion that her marriage was volatile and difficult, but she accepted it and looks back on it with fondness. Her husband, Elliott, died in 1987 at the age of 60.

Whatever the problems, in Wealthy's mind they are now overladen by the good. She looks back at their retirement plans with nostalgia and says, "I guess it was just not meant to be."[24]

Perhaps, her name was a third portent. Her mother had said that someday she would live up to it. She feels she has.

"Wealthy, rich in friends and rich in health."[25]

"It looks funny on a paycheque."[26]

Nor does Wealthy panic. At the age of 72, the summer after *that night*, she and her eleven year-old grandson, Nathan, were at her isolated summer camp on Black Bay, Lake Superior, where she has a tomato garden. She saw forest fires moving towards them from two sides. She had no phone, no car and the camp was land-locked. Wealthy's transportation had been via the boat of a local fisherman from nearby Squaw Bay. What did she do? She took 47 photos of the fire, and prepared an escape plan. If a fire came too close, she and her grandson would canoe to an nearby island.

"I don't panic, I never have."[27]

When five fire rangers, alerted by the family, arrived dressed in full fire regalia, she was calmly picking rocks with her grandson.

"I've had so many interesting things happen, it wouldn't do for me to panic."[28]

Her blonde daughter-in-law, Sharon Dawson, with steady blue-black eyes, frankly admits she feels she is the opposite.

"I'm not usually a calm person. I'm the kind that gets hysterical and isn't able to get a handle on things."[29]

However, her assessment of herself may be too harsh. On the night of the rescue she stayed steady, calming ChunAe Kollars, not panicking herself. Her survival pattern in their 24 hours-a-day business seems to have been one of assertive conciliation.

"A lot of people say to me that they could never work with their husband. But, like I say, it didn't happen overnight. It wasn't easy. I quit on him many times. I mean I quit. And I went to the unemployment office to get another job. But now it's come to the point where we both know what our jobs are and we have kind of learned to work it out together. We are more like partners even though I don't actually have any part of either business. But he does treat me as an equal."[30]

Husband Gerry agrees.

"My wife Sharon is my right hand man."[31]

"Sharon does more than any woman could, looking after two businesses, dispatching tugs, linesmen and divers, as well as our children's schedules. And, she doesn't even take Geritol!"[32]

Ten years into their marriage was a turning point. They had purchased the family business from Gerry's father four years after they were married. At that time Sharon went to work for her husband. They celebrated their tenth anniversary with a party on the Welcome Ship, inviting family and business people when, in fact, it was their worst year ever.

"I thought if we're going to go out, we're going to go out with a bang. We're going to celebrate the ten years we've had and if we go under, so be it. At least, we celebrated what had happened. Things did turn around after that and things did get better."[33]

However, Thunder Bay harbour has seen steady decline. For instance,

"In 1970 there was 23 operating terminals and right now we're down to seven."[34]

It was at the ten year point that Sharon realized her marriage had to change too.

"I'm the one behind the scene that does everything. Gerry is the one in front. I'm the one that gives the orders, I guess. We are on call 24 hours-a-day and we have a phone in the house and I have a home office. If I leave the phone, I have to make sure it's covered. I do all the books on the computer for both companies, Thunder Bay Marine and Thunder Bay Tug. Dispatch the tugs, the linesmen, you know, take any orders that come in for diving jobs or whatever. It's high pressure really. You can't leave that phone and that's what I found really hard, especially with young children, to be tied to that phone and not even be able to go for a walk around the block.

"There was a point in our marriage when things were kind of rough. I just felt there had to be a better way to have a relationship."[35]

Through brief counselling, at first together, and then with Sharon alone, their marriage partnership melded.

"It was just amazing what happened to our marriage after that. We didn't need counselling anymore. As I changed, Gerry changed. He changed in so many wonderful ways and that's when I realized how much he really loved me. It's the best thing that ever happened to our marriage. Since then, it's gotten steadily more fulfilling and a much better relationship.

"I think what I had to learn to do was to give up some things, that I couldn't be superwoman and that I couldn't do everything perfectly. And once I realized that, and just realized I had to concentrate on the priorities, then I was able to cope with the role that I play."[36]

She recognized the demands of the job on Gerry. She realized he could not come home from the strain of work and plunge into household chores.

"So, I've learned to get outside help. Even as far as the lawn goes, I hire somebody to do that.

"Gerry loves *Hagar* and it's all about a Viking and his boat. That describes Gerry to a tee. I've always teased him that he loves his tugs more than me. He's always babying them. He's always much more worried about what happens to them than he is about anything at home. But, I've learned to deal with that. That's his business, that's his focus in life, his tugs and his business."[37]

She now has help with the ever-demanding phone—and she has a cleaning woman. She has staked off her sanity time.

"About 10, 10:30 at night, that's my time. I cut off everything I'm doing. I don't care what the house looks like or what has to be done. I turn off everything. I usually make myself a hot chocolate and I go up. I'm a magazine freak. I love *Canadian Living* and *Lake Superior Magazine*. That's my time.

"Gerry on the other hand is a night person and he likes to stay up and watch TV quite late. So, he sits down alone watching TV, so it's a bone of contention, but I told him, I need that time, that's the only time of the day I have on my own. I'm a morning person, I like to go to bed early and at 7 o'clock my alarm clock wakes me up and I'm out of bed and busy."[38]

What do they do for entertainment?

"As a family, during the shipping season, it's difficult to find family time. If we do find it, we usually try to get away from the phone, and of course, we have our cellulars, but we escape out to camp, do something with the kids. Or just go for drives. We like to take them down to Marina Park and walk. We do pretty low key things with them.

"As far as Gerry and I are concerned, our favourite place is to go to Kangas Sauna. We find it is the only place where we can sit in silence and talk. During shipping season, this is one of our favourite things to do is to come and have a sauna and go for a drink or whatever.

"The kids love winter. We're winter people. That's the time when Daddy is finally around. So, we do a lot more with them, snowmobiling, cross-country skiing, we do a lot, we go out to camp and spend a lot of time there, just to get away. Both boys are into hockey, but especially Davis. Gerry coaches their hockey teams, that's what he does over the winter. They enjoy that. What we try to do every winter is to go on dates with the kids. They just love it when Daddy takes them for a date, each of them individually. They get to choose what they do for the evening and they just go with Daddy and do something special. I do it, too, but it's not as special because they see me all the time. But they just love their time with Daddy."[39]

Does Sharon feel the magnetism of Lake Superior like Gerry?

"Not really. I was raised on an inland lake. Lake Superior frightens me. Gerry will tell you I am not a very brave boater. I like it inside the breakwall. I get a

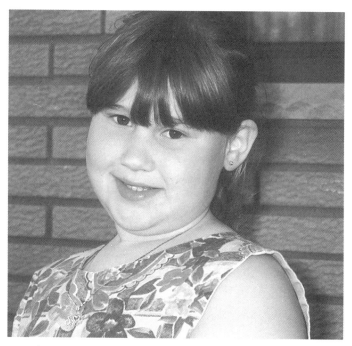

Heather Dawson wants to help people.

Nathan Dawson, left, wants to drive a tug like his Dad. Davis wants to be a professional hockey player.

little nervous outside the breakwall. But I love water. I just love the water, same with Gerry, we could never live on the prairies. I love looking at the Lake, especially when you come over Red River Road and see the harbour and the boats. I just find it so calming. We go out to my Mom's camp at One Island Lake, about 20, 25 minutes, go out for the evening for a swim, sauna and supper. So peaceful out there by the water. I love it, but I have a healthy respect for it.

"Those that don't have a respect are the ones that Gerry picks off the breakwall or has to go rescue here or there."[40]

Both Wealthy and Sharon have found their own way to cope, adapt, and enjoy the non-routine, the on-demand roles, characteristic of their 24 hour-a-day lives, Wealthy in retrospect, Sharon in the present. Nine-to-five husbands, with evenings and weekends free, regular social events, evening meals together, was and is something they only read about.

"I like to think it's my *SISU* that gets me through what I do. *SISU* is the stuff that gives you the courage to keep going, to keep your outlook bright and to take the optimistic view."[41]

The third woman in Gerry Dawson's life is only a girl. It is his daughter, Heather, eight years of age and in Grade 3.

"I'd like to be a dentist or a hairdresser or a doctor, someone to help people."[42]

It seems to run in the family. Heather has absorbed the family philosophy of trying to give back to the world some of the good they have been fortunate enough to reap.

Gerry Dawson and his family are a contrast to the usual portrayal of a sailor's life. Gerry as an individualistic but caring husband and father, Wealthy and Sharon as gutsy home and business managers, Heather, Nathan and Davis as healthy, productive children are not characteristic of the stereotypical rough-and-tumble waterfront scene. Is it the people, Thunder Bay, or the northern life-style which has made the difference?

*This sea and this sky were open to me...there was a sign, a call in
them–something to which I responded with every fibre of my being.*

It may be female chauvinism to select Inga Thorsteinson
as the focus of attention on the Canadian Coast Guard role
in the rescue from *Grampa Woo*—but Inga Thorsteinson is
special. Not only is she special, she is representative, a
seeming contradiction.

As a Search and Rescue (SAR) Seaman, she is representative of the three-person *Westfort* crew, which also included SAR Seaman Willie Trognitz, and Chief Coxswain Bob
King. All were equally dedicated to their job as they tena-
ciously stuck to their duties during the *Grampa Woo* "situation," despite conditions so dangerous the Rescue Coordination Centre in Trenton said they could leave, and despite
an earlier directive that said icing conditions on this coastal
rescue vessel created threatening conditions.

Inga is representative of the crew's cohesiveness under
pressure, their confidence in their ability and, oddly enough,
in their boat and their driving love of the sea.

Picture a little girl living on the banks of the Red River
in Manitoba. There were many Thorsteinsons of Icelandic
origin who sailed on Lake Winnipeg, but none, except her
father, Marvin, directly traced as a relative. Inga swam and
fished and played with boats. Her father always seemed to
be building or repairing a boat in the backyard.

"His joy is in the building and in the constructing
and as soon as that's finished, he sells it and buys
another one. What did my father do? That was always

During her early career, Inga Thorsteinson worked on the berthed museum ship, *Nonsuch*, during the off-season when she was not crewing on the *Lord Selkirk*. She still returns to Winnipeg to do rigging refits and maintenance work on the *Nonsuch*.

a mystery to me. My mother told me he was an inventor."[1]

While her father worked on his boat, Inga was repairing an old rowboat that she had found in one of the infamous Red River floods, often called the Red Sea.

"One year when the water was high and when I was a kid, I'd hang around the riverbank watching, and I'd have a boat hook and my rubber boots and I saw these gunwales floating by so I chased it down the river all through people's backyards until this thing drifted into shore and I pulled it up and hauled it home and my Dad helped me. I put new caps on the gunwales—it actually had maple flooring—I reinforced the frames inside and everything. It was a beautiful boat."[2]

Her first boat, claimed, repaired, and named *Bullhead* by Inga. It rests beside her father's *Lady Nane* in the backyard of the family home on the Red River where she grew up.

She called it *Bullhead*. For tenacity. It was the *Bullhead* that provided her entré onto a full-size ship.

"Every time the tour boat would run by, I would get out in my rowboat and start racing them. The passengers just loved that. They would be taking pictures and the Captain would throw me a bag of chips or some pop. I didn't twig on at the time but he was actually slowing down so that I could beat him. At the end of the season, I went to thank this nice guy who had been throwing me chips all summer and he let me steer the river boat. I started to cut school so that I could steer the river boat. This was a 150 foot long, 400 passenger ship. It wasn't a little boat. It was called the *River Rouge*."[3]

It was her rowboat *Bullhead* that provided her with her closest experience with the legendary Icelandic clairvoyance. When she left home to follow her career, the boat sat

It was the *River Rouge* that stirred Inga Thorsteinson's heart towards the sea when she skipped school to steer it. It is docked in front of the *Lady Winnipeg* at the Louise Bridge on the Winnipeg River.

Marvin Thorsteinson, Inga's father, in one of his favourite places, the garage, behind his home.

in the family backyard, gradually disintegrating. One spring, her father decided to burn it with the rest of the spring trash.

> "He saved the stern actually. I still have the stern sitting in my kitchen."[4]

The night of the burning, Inga's father lay awake thinking about Inga's boat—and Inga, miles away in Thunder Bay, caught his thoughts in a dream. Icelandics are noted for their prescience and clairvoyance. Some will say they can actually see a black halo around the head of an individual in trouble.

> "It was a very super-vivid emotional dream—I can't remember exactly what it was, but it was very disturbing to me—and I phoned him up the next day and said: 'Gee, you wouldn't know what I dreamed about last night. I dreamt about the *Bullhead* and I dreamt about you...and you know, it was a pretty intense dream.' And he said, 'That's funny, I burned almost all of your boat yesterday.' That is the closest I've ever come to a kind of weird connection."[5]

The *Bullhead* rose from its ashes into Inga's second boat, a 25 foot steel hull boat built in the Fifties with the original flathead, six cylinder Chrysler marine engine in it. Yes, it is called *Bullhead* and yes, it was rebuilt by her father. It was hauled by flatbed truck to Mission Island, Thunder Bay.

> "It's not what you call a yacht. It's kind of rough around the edges, but I have a lot of fun with it, mostly just trying to fix it."[6]

Recently, she acquired the *Freyr*, a hand-made 'cosine wherry'—or rowboat—that is only 13 feet long and 150 pounds. It will carry three times its weight. Its design dates back to the wherries used in the Seventeenth and

Eighteenth centuries as water taxis on the River Thames. The race for customers gradually expanded into the sport of sculling.[7]

The *Freyr* truly befits being named after the Norse god of fertility and wind. Inga specifically mentions that ships are not always female. Its hull is primarily cedar strips with inlays of two shades of Indiana walnut in an ornate sunburst pattern. It has fibreglass overtop and mahogany thwarts—seats—and eight and-a-half foot, spoon-bladed, spruce oars with brass tips and leather collars.

As Inga romps in her rowboat in a "pretty good chop" at the mouth of the McKellar River that empties into Thunder Bay harbour, she has often been offered help by other boaters—and even has had distress calls to the Coast Guard made about her. Despite her competence, even in the rowboat she carries a radio.

"VHF ship-to-shore radio. Everybody uses them."[8]

With Inga's soul encoded by water and boats, she was impelled to work on the water, male domain or not.

Consequently, within the special crew of the *Westfort*, Inga herself is special. Why? Because she is a woman. Of the approximate 208 permanent Search and Rescue employees in Canada, only eight are women. "There are not a lot of applications by women," Greg Sladics of the Canadian Coast Guard Office at the Sarnia Regional office said.[9] Considering the pioneering by Dorothea Dix for a life-saving unit for Sable Island around the turn of the Nineteenth century, which became the basis of the Coast Guard,[10] the minority role of women here is somewhat ironic.

The only Search and Rescue unit of the Canadian Coast Guard on the north shore of Lake Superior employs one woman: Inga. It has five other permanent employees. The base is located at Thunder Bay. At the eastern end of the Lake, 360 miles away, Sault St. Marie has its own volunteer, non-profit, Sault Search and Rescue, with training provided by the Canadian Coast Guard and the Canadian Armed Forces.

The Inshore Rescue Boat Program which employs university students has a more balanced gender ratio.[11] On the American south shore of Lake Superior, there are presently 11 Coast Guard bases, with eighty SAR employees, of which only one is female.[12] Before the U.S. Coast Guard was formed in 1914, there was a Life Saving Service that actually patrolled the beaches watching for shipwrecks.[13] It is unlikely any women were employed.

Inga is special, not only because she is working in a male domain, but also because she has worked largely without the complaints of harassment endured by many other women who seek to follow their bent, whether or not it runs afoul of gender taboos. In the mid Nineteen-Nineties, Leading Seaman Katherine McLeod, posted in Halifax, told the House of Commons Defense Committee that she wanted to end her seven year career with the navy because of sexual harassment.[14] In the historically male-dominated edifice of mariners, even the language provides a constant and unconscious gender barrier, just as some nautical slang could provide a racist barrier. Ms. McLeod was a Leading *Seaman*.

Inga Thorsteinson is a Search and Rescue *Seaman*. Yet, Inga's drive was stronger than any terminology, stronger than her guidance counsellor or her mother.

"Back in those days—that was in the late Seventies—there wasn't really a lot of women working on the water. I remember asking the guidance counsellor at school about going to the Coast Guard College and she said, 'No. You don't want to do that. You be a nurse or a teacher or something like that. They don't accept women at the Coast Guard College.'"[15]

Nevertheless, Inga worked summers on the *Lord Selkirk* on Lake Winnipeg. As her rank and responsibilities increased she quit university—and her mother kept bugging her to get *a real job*.

But the thrust of her life did not permit it.

While she worked on the *Lord Selkirk* in the summer, she worked on the berthed museum ship, *Nonsuch*, during the rest of the year.

"She's a two-masted square-rigged ketch, mid-Seventeen century coastal cargo ship originally built in England.[16] She was a working replica, kind of like the *Bluenose*. It sailed around the coast of England and France and that, and then crossed the ocean on the deck of a cargo ship and sailed around the Great Lakes. It came to Thunder Bay, and then it went on to sail the west coast. After that was all finished, the Hudson's Bay Company berthed it permanently in Winnipeg. I was Shiphusband, an old term for Shipkeeper. I was in charge of rigging maintenance and the historical interpretation of the vessel and giving public tours and stuff like that."[17]

Her relationship with the vessel continues and she recently has gone back to do a rigging refit and other maintenance work. Much as she loved this ship, she yearned for more. With a leave of absence, she sailed on the Atlantic Ocean on the three-masted topsail schooner, *Alexandria*. On it, everything was done manually.

"Our heat was provided by a wood stove in the room quarters. The Captain had an oil burner in his cabin. The food was kept in a great big wooden ice chest on board the deck, and when the ice melted, that was it for fresh food. Fresh water was rationed, and we bathed in sea water."[18]

The *Alexandria* was involved in the celebration in Quebec for a Jacques Cartier anniversary.

"Everybody's personal space, and what they expect out of a job, has changed. It used to be that you went onto a boat and you didn't expect to have your own private room. You just sort of assumed you were going to be living with three other guys or something. But now, everybody's personal space has changed. You used to crawl into your bunk with your clothes on and just your seaboots off and your coat. You'd change your clothes every once in a while when you chose the opportunity but everybody behaved like that and it was just standard. Nobody was really obsessed with privacy. You can't really be obsessed with privacy when you're on a boat anyways. Except for your bunk. If anybody sits on your bunk, this is a really big deal. That's your space."[19]

With her accumulation of sea time on the *Alexandria*, she went to Marine School in Winnipeg to get her Commercial Ships Officer licence.

Inga raced the *River Rouge* in a rowboat when she was a girl and then returned to it as Captain.

"At one time, Winnipeg was considered an inland commercial waterway and they had quite a bit of commercial shipping there. I came in on the very tail end of it. We were the last class and I was the first woman to graduate in Manitoba as a Master Minor Waters. So I got my ticket and was recruited out of Marine School to go and be the Second Officer on the old *Lord Selkirk* again. I didn't have my driver's licence yet. I could steer a fifteen hundred ton ship, but I couldn't drive a car. I would have been 24 or 25."[20]

She moved up to become First Officer on the *Lord Selkirk,* and then went back to the *River Rouge* as Captain.

"Ironically, the old Captain that was there originally and threw me the bags of chips all those years ago said, 'Well, it's come to this, eh?' It was great."[21]

She was working a 75 to 80 hour week with no overtime pay and no days off from May to November. When she heard rumours of possible layoffs because of the riverboat companies' being in trouble, she put in her application with the Coast Guard. Inga left Winnipeg to begin wheeling on the *Woodland,* which sailed out of Thunder Bay carrying craft paper, deck cargo and lumber down to the Detroit-Windsor area. Then, she was hired by the Coast Guard.

"I lucked into the Coast Guard job and I certainly have no regrets about that. That was spring '89. When the competitions came up, I was working as hard as I possibly could. Fortunately, I got in. With Bob King's help, I was sent on the coxswain's course. That was a bit of a feather in my cap. Now, we are one of the very few crews in Canada, maybe the only crew in Canada, where everybody is a trained coxswain on the crew. We're really unique that way."[22]

This uniqueness may have contributed to their survival *that night*. Each was able to take the wheel and spell the other off, each knew the ship and had confidence in it, despite its propensity to roll, its sluggishness from ice and its loss of buoyancy. Each had confidence in the ability of the others. Willie Trognitz noted:

> "We took turns on the wheel and I must say that we all worked together as a team and at one time I'd be on the wheel and Inga would be on the radar and Bob out a little crack would be watching which way the waves would be coming and he would say, 'Okay, hard to starboard. Hard to starboard!' because when the waves were coming from behind us, we'd want the wave to hit our stern flush on. We didn't want to be in a trough. A couple of times when we couldn't see a thing—you couldn't help it—the waves were coming from differ- ent directions—you'd be in a trough and then you'd get a real violent pitch and you were wondering if you were going to go over.

> "Like, we were in a pretty bad situation ourselves but holding our own. Nobody panicked or anything because we, you know, we've been in tight situations before."[23]

So the three worked in the close quarters of a wheel- house roughly the size of a large shower stall, trying to maintain the stability of the ship, shouting over the noise of the engines and the wind, unable to use the headphones needed during communication, grabbing at the handles for balance, passing around a two litre bottle of Coke as they became dehydrated and hoarse, their feet leaving the deck with the bunt of each wave; Inga seasick into a wastebas- ket the first time in her life, no-one noticed; Bob not feel- ing so well either, Willie having a bout of nausea, each tak- ing a turn watching out the back for the direction of the waves, the windows were iced from freezing spray, each taking a turn studying the radar, then wheeling.

Crewman Willie Trognitz, Chief Coxswain Bob King and Crewman Inga Thorsteinson in front of CCGC *Westfort*.

In order to stand off or station keep while the *Glenada* was conducting the rescue, the *Westfort* actually had to turn around a dozen or so times in what is called a 'pass track' to maintain its position. This meant being momentarily broadside to waves that were twice the height of the vessel. Even non-sailors know the threat to a ship when it is broadside to the waves.

Designed with a round, self-righting hull, the *Westfort* is 44 feet long with a beam of 12 feet, eight inches. Its bow freeboard is six feet two inches, and stern freeboard is four feet, seven inches. Its draft is three and-a-half feet. With 560 horsepower between its two engines, it has a maximum speed of 14 knots and a cruising speed of 9 knots. The hull is constructed of 3/16 inch Corten steel and is divided into nine watertight spaces.[24] In the wheelhouse are a radar, depth sounder, video plotter, differential GPS,

Loran C, Radio Direction Finder, two VHF radios, a radio with aircraft distress frequencies, a loud hailer, and two compasses, one gyro and one magnetic. The *Westfort,* painted a flashy red and yellow, is one of two Class 300 Search and Rescue Vessels in the Central and Arctic Region fleet. It is called a cutter, a generic term used in Canada for a Search and Rescue boat.[25]

Many who know the Lake feel the Coast Guard should not even have been out that night, considering the size of their vessel and the weather.

> "Like, that night—there was a prime example right there. That's what they're supposed to be doing is saving people like that. They've got the equipment supposedly to do it, that rescue boat? Like Gerry thought he was going to have to save them, too. Like, what's the use? Why are they there? All they are doing is costing you and I money."[26]

> "We were getting remarks from the guys on the ships saying, 'What are you doing out here? You guys better go home.'"[27]

These comments underline the *Westfort* crew's steadfastness to duty. Despite the unvoiced concerns each crewman might have had, the crew of the *Westfort* followed orders when tasked to attend the rescue. They competently handled their ship; they hung together not only to survive but to bring their ship home safely.

> "The worst thing I thought is we might have to, we might have to leave the scene. You know, we might have to run for cover. I certainly wouldn't have wanted to do that."[28]

The *Westfort* is used not only for rescue work, but also in buoy positioning, investigation of oil spills and pollution complaints mainly inside the harbour,[29] boat inspections, personnel transportation, missing persons, and water emergencies like the *Grampa Woo* rescue and other major marine incidents. Another Lake Superior Coast Guard vessel, the *Relite III*, is used for less demanding work. "The correct name for the unit is Rescue, Safety, and Environmental Response."[30]

During the boating season, the "weekend warriors" are a special problem dealt with by both the Coast Guard and the Coast Guard Auxiliary, knowledgeable volunteers with good boats.

"So what these folks, [the "weekend warriors"], have done is they come from the inland waters and they're dropping their boats off here and they're not as experienced as the people who actually leave their boats here in Lake Superior. These folks are real professional sailors. This is their Lake; this is their body of water and totally different. So the weekenders don't tend to be as well-equipped. You're talking about an inland sea here. All that applies on the ocean applies here. But some people are just used to Mud Lake or Shebandowan Lake or something, so they're here and all of a sudden the wind blows up and they're freezing and their motor breaks and they have no radio. So there's the difference."[31]

Bob King, Chief Coxswain, the one in charge, a fit-looking fifty, has been with the Canadian Coast Guard for 20 years, all spent in Thunder Bay. He has been with the Search and Rescue unit since 1980. His father was in the Coast Guard, and his son, Michael, also in the Coast Guard at the base in Thunder Bay, follows in their wake.

"For every hour on the boat, I spend two hours doing paper work. And, if you buy something, you have to record it half a dozen times. It just goes on and on. This kind of stuff really gets on my nerves and causes me a lot, a hell of a lot, more stress or anxiety than any call in the middle of the night."[32]

"It would be nice if we could just drive the boats and rescue the people, you know. But the first day that I joined, Bob says, 'Remember, going out and rescuing people is Number Two. Number One is the paperwork.'"[33]

Nevertheless, Willie Trognitz, 43, smiles like the Cheshire cat on the job. He can maintain the stability of a boat in waves just as if the water were calm.

"It's an honourable living. You'll never get rich while you're working for any branch of the government, but it's rewarding in its ways. Like a lot of my friends, they have good jobs and they work in elevators and mills and stores, they make a decent living. But, the excitement, the fresh air, the chance to work out on Lake Superior is so rewarding and exhilarating. I love it. I think it's great. I'm sure sometimes you're waiting for a disaster to happen, and sometimes, if you think about it, it can kind of bother you. Well, tonight's the night, or whatever. But, I don't usually think about it. I'm used to it now. If it happens that you've got to go out on a stormy night, well... But other times it happens that we got to go out on a night that there's a full moon and there's stars and not a ripple on the Lake and I think, jeez, I'm getting paid right now and it's a moonlight ride! I don't like the seasonal aspect. We work from April to the beginning of December. To be off work for three and-a-half to four months, I don't like that. But, you've got to take the good with the bad. Getting a job with the Coast Guard? Our base manager, George, [Stieh] would say, 'You've got as much chance as walking on the moon.'"[34]

In the marine business, Willie started at the bottom, working in an eight foot ditch tightening bolts in the ship

Ed Greer, Coxswain of the alternate crew of CCGC *Westfort* and husband of Inga Thorsteinson.

yards on Thunder Bay harbour. His mentor and employer, Fred Broennle, advised him to get his Dive Ticket, then to go to Marine Navigation School at Confederation College, now a discontinued course, where he received his Masters Certificate. When an opening came up in the Coast Guard, he jumped at it and has been there for eight years. His speciality is instruction in the handling of the Coast Guard's fast response, highly manoeuvrable vessel, a 26 foot Zodiac called the *Mark VII*.

"It's got twin 150 horsepower engines."[35]

"It will go through almost anything. If it does puncture one of the tubes, they have five different compartments so you're not in any real problem. If the boat does capsize, we have an airbag in the back which will right the vessel again."[36]

Both Willie and Inga have St. John Ambulance Advanced Level training. Inga is an instructor for the Rescue Specialist program.

The on-call crew live in a trailer on the waterfront near Keefer Terminal on 24 hour-a-day duty. The coxswains rotate every two weeks, the crew every week; Ed Greer, Inga's husband, takes over from Bob King; Terry Nuttall and Bill Southcott take over from Inga and Willie.

Inga, 37, has been a sailor for 18 years. In only one place of employment has she experienced the harassment or gender attention experienced by so many other women. She declines to go on record.

"I was really fortunate, even working with all these companies and private industry and that, the people I've worked with are just fantastic. I've only once had a problem. I was just very lucky almost the whole time."[37]

Inga lives in the confines of a small trailer with men, works with men, has been employed by men, yet the only gender issue she will talk about involved an interview for the position of Second Officer on the *Lord Selkirk*. Instead of asking her anything about her experience handling a ship and its crew, the ship's owner asked about her willingness to dress up in a special uniform. Later on he commented, "Inga, Inga, nice girl. She doesn't wear make-up."[38]

She does not wear make-up because it is not her style. Seeing the work place as gender-neutral, she has degenderized what many woman would kill for, nordic, aquiline features, a slender, lithe body, and natural ash-blonde hair. She is all business, except when she thinks of her husband Ed, or her dog Pongo, or her work, or the Lake or the *Freyr* or boating lore. Her eyes come alive. Then, she is back to business.

How does she account for surviving and thriving in a profession still largely male-dominated?

"I've always been really irritated if somebody has tried to make special allowance for me. That would really irritate me. I can remember when I first started sailing and first started wheeling, part of our job was hauling all of our passengers' luggage on board. If you get 130 passengers onboard and all of their luggage for a week, that was part of a deckhand's job—to haul it up to everybody's cabin. Sometimes you get a new deck-hand who'd get all upset if he saw me carrying a

Solitary bow watch on the *Alexandria*, in Black Diamond foul weather gear, symbolic of Inga Thorsteinson's wish to be herself.

couple of suitcases. I found that if I pulled my weight to the best of my ability, then I don't have any problems with the guys but if I start looking for favours and thinking, well, I can't do this because I think I'm smaller or I'm lighter, then there will be a bit of resentment if you let that start."[39]

What Inga would never say, but others do, is that she is excellent in her job and a hard worker. She has put in long hours with no over-time and has always tried to learn. But Inga downplays her uniqueness.

"Oh, there's a few of them, women. There's more and more all the time. When I go down to Cornwall next week, there's going to be a woman there who's actually been sailing longer than I have."[40]

In fact, it was a female American Coast Guard coxswain at a training session in Sydney, Nova Scotia, that taught Inga many of the manoeuvres she used *that night*.

"I'm not sure gender's more of an issue or less of an issue. I'm still trying to figure that out. But I guess as long as gender is raised as an issue, it still is."[41]

Gender is not an issue nor is the terminology, in what Gerry Dawson says about Inga:

"She's one hellava boatsperson. She has a Master Minor Waters Certificate. She does a lot of the engineering. She's as good on a boat as anyone else I've worked with."[42]

5 ~ THE CREWS AND THE SHIPS

We exist only in so far as we hang together.

Gerry Dawson is "The Head." Jack Olson is "The Heart." And, Jim Harding is "The Limbs." The tugboat, *Glenada*, functions like an organism. Like an ant hill or a bee hive, better than planet Earth, but essentially the Gaia theory in microcosm; nothing functions on its own, something as large as Earth may be a "living creature."[1]

Unwittingly, the crew jokes along these lines. The men began calling Gerry "The Head" because he always hangs his head out the window to get a better view. Tacitly and overtly, they recognize the metaphor is accurate. They know that Gerry is the Captain, the brains, the discipline, the ultimate bearer of responsibility, even though he does not act it.

"You really have a tendency to forget that Gerry owns the tug, you know, because there's none of this pushing this, or I'm the boss and you're the so and so. We have a hell of a good time when we're out there together, lots of laughing and joking and that."[2]

Jack, as chief engineer, "the only engineer,"[3] keeps the throb of the engines steady and the boat functional. Without "The Heart," it would die.

"That's Chief Engineer Doctor Jack Olson. Cardiologist. I like that."[4]

Jim is "The Limbs," the hands and arms and feet. He wears running shoes and uses them. His tall, rangy form can be seen loping from the parking lot to the ship. He

Gerry on land is just a regular guy. Gerry at sea is the master of his ship, even though he doesn't act it.

Chief Engineer, Jack Olson, always a twinkle in his eye.

Crewman Jim Harding makes fast the *Glenada's* working line until the *Helena Oldendorff's* mooring lines are secured.

runs around the ship. There, he is always on his feet, tying up, moving lines, watching, wheeling, helping with the engine, sometimes diving. Some call him "Tarzan"[5]—a blue-eyed, black-bearded Tarzan—as he handles the lines from the salties like vines, looking as if he is ready to swing out on them and yodel the Tarzan cry. Ah-uh-ah-uh-ah.

One of the main tasks of the two tugs in Thunder Bay Tug Services, the *Glenada* and the *Point Valour*, which Gerry co-owns with Rolland (Rollie) Frayne, is to move ships. They mainly move salties—ocean-going ships—because these huge vessels are not nimble enough to negotiate their length between loading docks or through the breakwall of the harbour. Although usually longer, lakers can manage on their own, except when the weather is bad, as it was on *that night*, October 30, 1996. In storms and in ice, they need the help of tugs. Two tugs working together push and pull to manipulate the bulk of the ship onto the correct course. Alternately taking turns with the only other tug company on the harbour, Thunder Bay Tug Services moved 360 ships in 1996, although the number varies from year to year. As well, both tugs clear elevator slips of ice, and work with the Coast Guard on rescues. Their working year is roughly between March and December, depending on the ice in the Lake.

The three tugs in Gerry's other company, Thunder Bay Marine Services, take pilots out to ships, do charters, are the central nervous system of pollution abatement in the harbour, move ore, also clear elevator slips of ice, contract diving jobs, and conduct special tours.

Although a tug working at night looks like an ethereal firefly flitting about on the water, it generally has little mystique. In reality, a tug is the German Shepherd of the sea, working, saving lives, sniffing out trouble, always loyal to its task.

The crew has not said it, but "The Body" of their anatomical working unit is the *Glenada*. It is a fifty year-old tug— "tugs last forever"[6]—which Gerry bought in partnership

The *Glenada*, a 76 by 25 foot tug, built in Owen Sound about fifty years ago, was purchased by Gerry Dawson and Rolland Frayne in 1995.

with Rolland Frayne in 1995. When the boiler had broken down on the companies' only tug, the ocean vessel *Point Valour*, Gerry had to cancel a trip to a conference at the Marine Club in Toronto. The word went out at the conference that Gerry was looking for a tug. Jack Purvis from the Sault called to say the *Glenada* was for sale.

Gerry did not know "whether it was strange or meant to be," but the *Glenada* was acquired because of the broken boiler and cancelled trip. Ironically, the *Point Valour* is still going strong.

The *Glenada*, 76 feet by 25 feet, was built in Owen Sound and named after a town in Manitoba. Originally, it was permanently based in Liverpool, Nova Scotia, as part of the Royal Canadian Navy fleet, with a crew of 12. Thunder Bay couple, Jean and Howard Dowswell, held their wedding reception on the *Glenada* in 1944. At that time, Howard Dowswell was a petty officer in the Navy.[7]

In 1977, "the whole insides" of the *Glenada*, including the wheelhouse, were rebuilt, the beam widened by four feet, the length shortened by eight feet, and a new engine installed. The 3/8 inch hull is mild steel. Its D399

The tug, *Point Valour*, co-owned by Gerry and "Rollie," is part of the Thunder Bay Tug Services.

Caterpillar engine has 1250 horsepower and maximum revolutions per minute of 1200. It can tow a 30,000 DWT ship with a speed of six or seven knots. With a maximum speed of 12 knots, and two diesel generators, a GM 67kw and a VM 43 kw, the *Glenada* draws eight and-a-half feet of water. Its gunwhales, its railings, are 11 feet off the water at the bow and six feet off the water at the stern. In the stern quarter, about seven feet of the bulwarks—the sides—are open for drainage.

"The deck level is only eight inches above the water at the stern end. So the waves are twenty feet above that at times and Gerry, to maintain his station, would sometimes back up, and the boat would start to climb and then a wave would just break over the top and fill up that stern deck until it would flood. I kept floating around back there."[8]

Inside the wheelhouse are two compasses, one gyro and one magnetic, two VHF radios, two radars, a GPS receiver, an electronic chart plotter, and two search lights. But what is most unique about the *Glenada* is the gear box. It has an hydraulic marine reverse gear with a three to one reduction, capable of reversing in two seconds.

"We got the only tug that's got a gear box that will switch from ahead to astern in two seconds. The *Point Valour* takes fourteen seconds."[9]

Both the *Glenada* and the *Point Valour* are plastered with fenders, enormous tires, along their sides and across the stern, the big bow tire giving the ship the look of a cruising mouth leaning forward with lips puckered into a seductive 'o.' Some say the tugs look like giant suckers up from the depths of the Lake bottom.

The spotlight, tires, and gear box, all played a definitive part, just as the men and the ship itself, just as the *McCarthy* and Lake Superior, played a definitive part in the drama near Thunder Cape *that night*. High tech was less important than seamanship.[10] Low tech, seamanship, and the Lake worked together.

"This outfit is great. When something like this came up, we had everything. The boat was in good shape. I know that. Because we keep it that way. We had full bunkers, we had grub and food. Everything's running mechanically well and we didn't have to worry about anything. About five o'clock they phone us again. Like I said, we were moving a boat and we didn't even have to come back to the dock. If anything happens, it won't be because of neglect. We never have to be out there and wish, gee, I wish I'd have a new fuel pump in."[11]

It had been four years since Jack Olson retired in his late fifties to work in his variety and craft store, AJ's Handcrafts, on Highway 61 south of Thunder Bay, owned by him and his wife, Joyce. With persuasion, Jack reluctantly agreed to be part-time engineer for Thunder Bay Tug Services' newly-acquired *Glenada*. On *that night*, he was 61 and had been on the Lakes for 39 years.[12] Stoutish and a little arthritic, he nevertheless took to the new job like a young man.

"My part-time job turned out to be pretty full. I like it here where I am. When I need a part to fix something, I go ahead and git it. These tugs are always A-One.[13]

"I would give you a thousand dollars for any tug you could find that supplies an exposure suit for each, like Jim had on that night, which was good that he had it. We've got life jackets. The biggest thing happens and you get into a problem: survival suit! It fits on over all your clothes. If the boat's going to be sinking, you just grab that on and zipper it and jump in. These are over 450 bucks apiece."[14]

The *Glenada's* fittings also include two radars, a microwave and a television set. It is dry-docked as required. Two years ago the propeller was replaced.

Jack's father had come from Norway on a cattle boat.

"That's my inheritance on the sea."[15]

Jobs were scarce in Thunder Bay and Jack headed for British Columbia. Dissatisfied, he returned to Thunder Bay where he found work on the waterfront.

"Out of desperation, I went to work on the boats. I started out firing and then I went oiling. And I thought if I'm going to do this crap, I might as well get my engineer's paper. And when I got my engineering papers, the money was pretty good, so I wasn't going to go back to driving truck. I just got third class. That's all I needed for what I wanted. That took about seven years. At one time, I was the youngest second engineer on the Great Lakes on the biggest boat, the *Algocen*."[16]

He grew up in Scobel Township outside Thunder Bay. What did his parents do? "Fight." How did they support themselves?

"You know, I don't know. I just don't know how they ever supported themselves. You're a kid and all you're interested in is getting something to eat."[17]

Jim Harding, 34, crewman, was born in Windsor and came to Lakehead University to study geology and then engineering. While working as a geo-technician geologist he heard about Gerry Dawson, who was then "towing silver ore off Silver Islet and bringing it to Thunder Bay to mill."[18] Silver Islet, back in the Eighteen seventies, was one of the richest silver mines in the world.[19] More than a hundred years later the Queen Charlotte Mining Company was hoping to plumb again some of that wealth. When Jim met his future wife, Meghan, he wanted less itinerant work and

The Dawson family tug, the *Rosalee D.*, at work loading tailings from the abandoned Silver Islet mine in Lake Superior.

asked Gerry Dawson for a job. Sharon had a good feeling about him.

"He just walked into our lives basically. It was serendipity. He just walked in and needed a job. I kept saying to Gerry: 'There's something about this guy: hire him. You need extra help.'"[20]

It worked out for Jim, too.

"It's a good relationship. I couldn't ask for a better one. I've not done anything that I have enjoyed as much as working with Gerry. It's very enjoyable, very diverse. Even the same things have to be tackled in different ways so there is always an element of problem-solving to everything that we go about. It's different every time."[21]

Gerry does not think of himself as "The Head." He often says:

"I don't feel that anyone works for me. I feel they

work with me.[22] Friends have become employees and employees have become friends."[23]

It was this bond that has inspired a determined loyalty and trust all round.

At the time of the rescue, Gerry was not even 40. Most people who know the story of October 30 expect to find a seasoned mariner, grizzled and lined from years of wind and sun, voice hoarse from competition with the waves. When they meet Gerry, they are taken aback at his youthful appearance and casual manner, his auburn hair untouched by grey, his figure slim, tenor voice soft, head-down, shy smile, and a seemingly non-assertive but confident manner. He has the reputation of being a good business person.

> "He is a good businessman—he always was—even as a kid, he used to charge me interest even if I borrowed five bucks from him."[24]

Gerry gives the credit to his wife, Sharon, for the business acumen in his two companies.

Sharon Dawson at the phone, in the nerve centre of their companies, Thunder Bay Marine Services and Thunder Bay Tug.

"Sharon is my right hand man. The anchor behind me. I don't think there's anything she doesn't do except go on the boats with me. She looks after the book work. She answers the phone pretty well day and night, dispatches the linesmen, more or less dispatches the tugs when they're needed, looks after the diving jobs."[25]

Besides their daughter, Heather, Gerry and Sharon have two sons, Nathan, ten and Davis, six. The family lives in a well-maintained mid-scale home in a family neighbourhood of Thunder Bay. Gerry has a sister, Cheryl, and three brothers. Stan is the Captain, and Glen, crewman, on the Buchanan Lumber Sales tug and barge, *Twolan*, which transports lumber down the Great Lakes. Richard works for the City of Thunder Bay and helps out Gerry on the tugs.

Socially, Gerry gets together with a group that he has hung with for over 15 years. He played hockey with them, and now hunts, fishes and snowmobiles with them, the men getting together with their wives for occasions like New Year's Eve, or steak and lobster at somebody's house.

Captain Stan Dawson, Gerry's brother and captain of the tug, *Twolan*.

For four years, he has hosted a Father's Day summer trip with the kids, no mothers.

> "Last year, we had 14 kids and nine fathers. We take the *Rosalee D* and then take a couple of small boats to go fishing.[26] I do it because I like to show them the Lake. That's the way my father was, too. It's as beautiful a country as anything you're going to find anywhere."[27]

He says he is "somewhat of a conservationist." When the group goes hunting, they set their own limit of two animals. What they take in with them, they take out. No littering. In fact, even while working, he'll clean up a site where garbage has been left.

When the shipping season closes, he coaches his sons' hockey team. As far as Davis is concerned, it is career training.

> "I would like to be a professional player in the NHL. I like boats too, especially when my Dad is driving cause he's so safe and I know the boat won't tip over because he'll just make it not, cause it never has before, has it, Mom?"[28]

As a child, math was Gerry's strong point. He hated reading, but nevertheless passed his Grade 13 only one credit short.

> "So the last year of high school was probably my party year. That's what my Dad figured. He used to say, 'What did you do? Just stay warm there for a year?' I did learn a lot. Chemistry I enjoyed."[29]

Although he too played hockey as a youngster, his main interest lay with the waterfront and boats.

> "Our summers were spent down at the ore dock where my Dad had the boats. We made money there. We used to collect scrap iron on Saturdays. In spring break and summertimes, we'd go down and pick up old

nails and things and scrap metal and make money that way. We were always there. I never had a social life in high school, probably not until about Grade 13, because every night after school, we used to do the linesman service—or I did when I was in high school—to buy my 'toys,' not a bad job for the money, Thunder Bay's version of longshoremen. I'd spend all my time after school, in spring and summer, with my Dad, running the tugs. In high school, I started. I was fifteen when I captained the tug the first time alone. So, I was always more or less career-oriented and family-oriented.

"I remember all the other kids used to say, 'Aren't you coming into town to the CLE, [Canadian Lakehead Exhibition] and stuff?' We didn't. We'd make our own fun out there. We'd go out to Pie Island and build a raft, play at lots of islands and have lots of fun. Did lots of hunting even in the summertime."[30]

He had no time for girls in high school. Sharon was his first girlfriend. When they met, it was an instantaneous attraction. Sharon went off to Carleton University in Ottawa but neither dated. Sharon left university and they married a few years later.

"I don't think they [Sharon's parents] wanted us together. 'You're not marrying a sailor? Are you out of your mind?' "[31]

Despite spending his spare time with his Dad and on the waterfront, Gerry is not a loner. "I enjoy having people around me and socializing."[32]

Although he does not look like an old salt, the years of experience are there. Right out of high school, he worked for his father and when the opportunity came to buy the family business in 1983, he did.

"My parents offered it to all my brothers and I was the only one that really wanted it. The rest of them didn't think their wives could handle it. So I ended up with it."[33]

By then he had four certificates under his belt, including the 350 Command Endorsement Certificate allowing him to captain a tug capable of towing a ship of any size anywhere around North America.

Gerry regards his father as a formative figure in his life.

"My father was a very tough person. He was a tough person to work for and work with, but he had the same feelings and he worked the same way I do. I don't expect anyone to do a job that I can't do. He was very strict and I respect him for it. It helped us a lot. I only got a chance to tell him that once. That was only about two weeks before he died. He kind of felt he hadn't done anything in his lifetime and I told him—I kind of laid it on the line—what he'd done for all of us at different points in our lives. I think a lot of it was our childhood, the way he brought us up, he was very strict, very disciplinary, and you never questioned him. He thanked me for it afterwards. It was good to finally get it off my chest. He died shortly after."[34]

Gerry always feels his presence.

"Every time I go out on the boat, I think he's with me. I do talk to him quite often when I'm on the boat or if I'm sitting out at the camp or something out at my Mom's camp looking out over the Bay."[35]

Sharon says Gerry is not as hard on people as his father was.

"Gerry has more patience. He doesn't mind stopping to teach, but once he does, he expects you to know it. He doesn't want to have to tell you again."[36]

Gerry always had to be "two steps ahead" of his Dad, and now crewman Jim is "two steps ahead" of Gerry.[37] Son, Nathan, is learning. He has been on the tug since he was four and is very comfortable there. Gerry thinks, "...it is in his blood and he's not going to change."[38]

"I love working around the tugs and helping my Dad around the dock. When I grow up I'd like to be a captain on a tug boat."[39]

Gerry regards himself as the kind of person who does not turn away from things, and who will stick to a job to the end, trying to do it as well as he can.

"There's so many things that have happened in my life and my parents' life on the Lake where you don't hesitate. If there's someone in danger, you do what you can for them. Maybe I've been lucky. I haven't had anything come back on me yet. But, there's lots of times I will refuse diving charters and things like that when I realize what the Lake is doing out there and I won't go out. I know when not to push the Lake."[40]

Gerry often thought about a rescue his mother told him about in which his father was involved.

"He was the only one who would go out that night and help those people."[41]

His mother, Wealthy, remembers it well.

"It was pouring rain and winds. They got a call or they heard calls of help down by the Provincial Mill in Thunder Bay here. Anyway, my husband got this call and it was just pouring and the winds were high and so anyway the Coast Guard were phoning around to see if they could get someone out, and right away Elliott got his gear on, and this fellow went with him and they were able to save two of those fishermen. The other one drowned. They had life jackets, but they were underneath the seat. That's when we had the Bum Boat and my husband outfitted them, boots right up to their caps, then we never did hear from the two that were saved, never heard a word. I have the letter yet for Elliott to be at the city council at such and such a night."[42]

Like the hero in his favourite book, *Hungry as the Sea* by Wilbur Smith—although not a reader, he does enjoy Wilbur Smith—Gerry is known for what he smokes, in Gerry's case cigarillos. However, he is mainly known as a non-smoker, and regards himself as a non-smoker, but concedes that when he smokes, it can be pack a day. He never smokes at home. While shrimp is his favourite seafood, he likes hamburgers and omelettes. The food he remembers from childhood are his Mom's Hawaiian ribs and Igloo cake, which she still makes for birthdays. His comfort food is popcorn. On board, he has the proverbial bottle of rum for the occasional snort when the day is done, which Jack says is never abused.

Gerry and his family attend Westminister United Church.

"I enjoy it. There's a really nice minister at Westminster, but she's not there as much anymore, and Rev. Peden, I really enjoyed him. He was a good influence."[43]

There is an underlying feeling of fatalism in the family, a feeling that things will work out, that "it was just meant to be."

"I don't know what the big picture is. Why all these things have come together for us. We've been very fortunate with the way things have worked for us. All these things seem to fall into place. At times, when we were almost destitute, a $30,000 or $40,000 job will come along and kind of bale us out at the right time. We've been very fortunate that way. I don't know why or what the purpose is."[44]

The small picture, though, is that three men working in sync, almost telepathically in tune with each other and in tune with their boat and the Lake, produce results. The business functions, each man is happy at his work, jobs big and small are accomplished, and their reputation is good. If the team had worked less harmoniously together, the precarious situation on *that night* might have taken a dramatically different turn.

"If Gerry couldn't just expect engines to work, then he could not with confidence have stayed out there. If I didn't know Gerry, I couldn't have done it. There's no way. I knew it was perilous, and that's what I'm saying that I'm not going overboard, but I knew what he could do to make sure that I wasn't going to go overboard. He had to know what I was doing, that I would not do anything that was going to unduly jeopardize myself, jeopardize the boat."[45]

Wilbur Smith said:

"In my stories, good triumphs over evil...And in the end, bravery, endurance, and courage carry the main characters forward."[46]

The story of *that night*, October 30, 1996, unlike the ordered reality of fiction, would be much more complex. The only evil, if it is evil, was the frailty of ships and humans.

It was as if I had jumped into a well–into an everlasting deep hole.

When the towline broke between the *Walter J. McCarthy Jr.* and *Grampa Woo*, the spirit of beauty, symmetry, and strength that seemed to sail with *Grampa Woo* in the first five months of its life as a cruise ship on Lake Superior, departed. It no longer had a symbiotic, mutually workable, relationship with its Captain, its Master, Dana Kollars. The ship had taken control, no longer a beautiful, compliant *she*, as Dana Kollars referred to her.

The spirit of ChunAe Kollar's father after whom the ship had been named, seemed to flee, perhaps to search for another way to save his daughter's husband.

Having grudgingly accepted the tow after two tries by the thousand foot *McCarthy* over three hours[1] in the wild conditions some seven or so miles offshore, *Grampa Woo* came along "like a well-trained dog,"[2] according to Captain Smyth. He was travelling about "eight miles per hour to avoid pulling the *Grampa Woo* under."[3]

However, once its leash snapped some four hours and fifteen minutes later,[4] the compliant ship changed. It was becoming unsteady with ice and snow. Completely out-of-control, it was swaying like a drunken hula dancer, keeping time with the swooping waves, free even from the extra sea anchors earlier deployed to keep it steady and pointed into the waves. Dana and crewman, Robin Sivill, were being flung from side to side, like wisps of grass on the hula skirt.

But *Grampa Woo* was no lovely Hawaiian hula dancer. *She* had become a sort of crazed creature, a wounded and ice-grizzled Moby Dick, unpredictable, suffering, and for the men inside, malevolent. It was threatening to capsize and drown them, to escape with them down the shipping channel and out to sea, or to self-destruct on the rocks of the Lake.

Robin and Dana were alone with this thing. The lights of the *McCarthy* and another laker, the *Oglebay Norton*, had disappeared into the roaring black after the bridle parted. They seemed to be moving towards shelter inside greater

Captain Dana Kollars, owner of the ill-fated *Grampa Woo*.

Grampa Woo, a harbourfront eye-catcher prior to *that night*.

Thunder Bay harbour, leaving Dana and Robin prey to the demented boat, but expecting help would be provided by the *Glenada* and *Westfort*.

Such a change had come over *Grampa Woo*. The sleek million dollar cruise ship had been white as a gull, its graceful lines flowing into the needle beak of a bowsprit. It had been christened *Grampa Woo*, 'Grampa The King,' after ChunAe Kollars' father whose untimely death from liver cancer occurred while he, and the whole family, waited in anticipation for the acquisition of the first *Grampa Woo*, purchased in 1992.[5] This smaller, ninety-two foot, forty-passenger ship was sold to the Apostle Islands Cruise Service Company, and the Kollars upgraded to the present *Grampa Woo*.[6] ChunAe's father was strong in his death, as he had been strong in his life, escaping Japanese pursurers by timing his jump from a moving train to land in a river that would break his fall and foil his captors. Naming the ships after her father kept him with ChunAe, and often she talked to him in her mind, especially *that night*.

"I say, okay, Dad, help me, and I asked God to help us, too."[7]

At 110 feet overall length, 98 gross tons, and certified to carry 150 passengers, *Grampa Woo* was strikingly bigger than most of the non-freighters on Lake Superior. Its gleaming white aluminum hull and luxury appointments made it an immediate eye-catcher. Originally a Crew Boat built to service oil rigs in the Gulf of Mexico, it was converted into a Head Boat after a few years and used for luxury "party-boat fishing on the Atlantic"[8] when Dana bought it.

Dana would not like to think that *Grampa Woo* had become an entity out of his control. In the back of his mind he was wondering, wondering, if he were to blame. Had he done something to let his ship down? Only after, when he had time to review the events, and the Coast Guard and his insurance company had investigated, would he really know.

At age 48, Dana's life had been a zigzagging trip up the ladder to the treasured existence he and his family had found on Lake Superior. Born into a relatively poor farm family in Nebraska, he "...went into a seminary and studied to be a priest for two years. [He] flunked celibacy"[9] and withdrew. Now, an ordained minister with several church affiliations, he is able to perform marriage ceremonies on his ship.[10] After the seminary, he attended the University of Nebraska and studied Agricultural Engineering. In his sophomore year, he was drafted into the army as a private, and was discharged 20 years later as a commissioned officer with the rank of major. He also attained his Coast Guard certification as a licensed captain.[11]

His life was veering away from agriculture, turning towards his childhood love of the water. He now has his Master of One Hundred Ton certification and is licensed in western waterways, the Great Lakes and Near Coastal.[12] On the *Grampa Woo,* he doubles as engineer.

Dana felt fortunate that his love of water, maybe from his Norwegian ancestry—not from his father who was afraid of water—his ability to deal with people and his business interest were all nurtured in the army. His command of two units in excess of one hundred people as well as his assignments on the Gulf of Mexico and the Pacific were especially helpful. He met his diminutive wife, ChunAe, in Korea. Dana, who speaks Korean as a second language, also knows classical Latin.

"We moved here to the North Shore [what Canadians call the West Shore] about nine years ago."[13]

Not only was there a bonding with his ship, and with his wife who worked along side him in their business, Lake Superior Excursions, and with the community, there was a bonding with his crewman, Robin Sivill. Both were military men, Robin an enlisted man in the British infantry, Dana a commissioned officer in the U.S. Army. Both were discharged on the same day of the same year, both have their birthday on the same day. Both had seen death. Robin had seen it in an anti-terrorist squad to which he was attached; Dana had faced it twice, once in a helicopter crash, once in

ChunAe Kollars, originally from Korea, inspired the naming of the *Grampa Woo*, a tribute to her father.

a hostage incident. Perhaps a third time, when he rescued a ship off Isle Royale.

Robin, an instructor of diving and a divemaster, met Dana while he was instructing and supervising diving at the "world famous deep freshwater wrecks" on the western shore of the Lake. Sporadic dive jobs with Dana worked into a full-time job when the second *Grampa Woo* was acquired. Robin now is full-time crewman and virtually lives on the boat. As his enthralment with the Lake developed, his marriage to a woman in St. Paul, Minnesota, more than two hundred miles away, faltered. Eventually they divorced and the Kollars became his family.

Robin has all the qualifications to take the exam for his captain's licence at the Coast Guard testing centre in St. Louis, Missouri, which he plans to do soon. Dana likes to have two licences aboard. His son, Clinton, who also has his Master of One Hundred Ton certification, "at one time the youngest licensed Master on the Great Lakes,"[14] works when necessary for his father, but wants to devote his time to his computer graphics business. The Kollar's daughter, Nina, also helps, but is following her star to Japan to teach English.

For the Kollars, it all began in the early morning hours of October 30, 1996, the day before Halloween. About four a.m., ChunAe and Dana were awakened by the sound of shrieking winds and thrashing trees. With maintenance work to be done, Dana decided he might as well get an early start. *Grampa Woo* needed to be readied for its long voyage to the Gulf of Mexico where its schedule of fall and winter cruises on the Illinois, Mississippi, Ohio, Tennessee and Tom Bigsby waterways would begin. He also wanted to check the boat because of the storm, although he knew the scope of the two ton, stainless steel mooring was more than adequate.

Grampa Woo was anchored some hundred miles north at Grand Portage, its last voyage completed for the season. It normally would have been off Lake Superior by now.

"Our departure from Lake Superior was delayed by the company that manufactured the propellers. They were supposed to have been delivered to us just after Labour Day, early September, and now as most of the

Robin Sivill, crewman on the *Grampa Woo*.

mid-west United States know, that delivery was over sixty days late. Were it not for that, we would have been off of Lake Superior a week ahead—two weeks ahead of the incident that took place. We took the propellers off after confirming with the company that in fact the propellers would be delivered the next day. Obviously, that confirmation was in error. Not only did it not arrive that Monday. It didn't arrive Tuesday or Wednesday or Thursday, when it was too late."[15]

Arriving at the protected harbour of Grand Portage about seven in the morning, Dana and Robin decided the waves were just too high to try to get out to *Grampa Woo* in their inflatable Zodiac.

"I really didn't want to get in that inflatable and go out to the boat that day. The waves were bad! And Dana, he said, '…we'll just get wet and do it, come on.' But, it's cold and miserable, Chief, I said. 'All right,' he said. 'Let's just go to the Lodge and have breakfast.' "[16]

On the way, Dana went to speak to C. "Keck" Melby, owner of Voyageur Gateway to Adventure Marina Motel, where Dana's ship was moored. Robin stayed to fuel the Zodiac. Next thing, Robin was running to Dana "with terror in his eyes"[17] and a string of expletives in his British infantry voice.

"I was kneeling down, watching the dock and looking up—and did a double-take on the boat and wow, that is moving! He kind of looks at me: 'No. You don't understand.' Which is true. I'm still learning a lot of things about big boats. But, I said: 'No, Chief. It's moving.' And then he came running down and realized that I was serious and then he saw it. And then, we just launched the Zodiac and there was no thought like shall we go or anything."[18]

They grabbed an extra anchor on the way to the dock. *Grampa Woo* seemed to have stopped drifting. The anchor had caught again.

When the two men stepped into the Zodiac, they unknowingly stepped into what might have been an everlasting hole of helplessness and despair. Because of assistance, the seemingly everlasting hole would only last three days.

The loss of control began immediately. On their way to the drifting ship, the engine of the Zodiac began to sputter.

> "I was concentrating on watching where the *Woo* was going and thinking of what we had to do and Dana said to me: 'Get the oars out.' And, I'm looking at him like, what? He said: 'Get the oars out,' and I thought well, ya, it's a joke, right?"[19]

It was no joke. Something was wrong with the engine of the Zodiac. Facing them was the open water of Lake Superior and their increasing vulnerability to the waves. Their course would take them right past the *Grampa Woo*, past the entrance to the harbour, out into open water and, eventually, the rocks of Isle Royale, some 20 miles away.

Immediately Dana and Robin recognized their peril.

Both men were totally soaked. They had no protective clothing, no radio, and were in an uncovered boat. Worst of all, no-one knew they were adrift. For all anyone knew, they were doing maintenance work on the *Grampa Woo*.

> "The wind was blowing so that had we not been able to catch the *Grampa Woo*, we would have been blown out to sea. And no-one would have known that. To be caught on that Lake in a small, uncovered vessel with no radio..."[20]

In the three-day saga, this was one of the two moments of greatest despair for both men.

They would survive to experience the second moment of great despair. Dana coaxed the dying engine to propel the Zodiac towards *Grampa Woo*; Robin tied a long bow line around his waist and leaped across the waves to the big ship. Now a whole new set of problems faced them. First, they must try to secure the ship. They deployed a second anchor and ground tackle.

"Hopes were that with the second anchor and with the increased scope on the mooring, that we would be able to stay on mooring until the winds subsided."[21]

His computation indicated the steel mooring weighed 3,560 pounds.

"The weight of our mooring and the scope we used exceeded the tables for holding the vessel. We had approximately 180 feet of line and we were in 17 feet of water which gave us a seven to one scope, which was more than adequate for a mooring consistently of 3,000 to 4,000 pounds of steel with welded raybars for additional holding power."[22]

Neither he, nor anyone, could have reckoned with the force of the wind.

"The state of Minnesota in that area received on the day her lowest barometric pressure reading and that barometer reading was equivalent to those recorded in the eyes of hurricanes and that's a matter of record with the National Weather Service.

"The wind was so strong that it was lifting the water right off the surface of the Lake. That happens a lot, but in this case, the water was so thick you couldn't see the shoreline. When that wall of water hit us, we could feel it move us physically."[23]

"The last time Dana checked the fathometer when the ship was holding, it showed they were in 38 feet of water.

"If she slipped any more and the water got any deeper, we were gone."[24]

The ship slipped. They were gone. The *Grampa Woo* was drifting out. During all this, Dana had radioed Keck Melby at the motel, the Canadian Coast Guard and Thunder Bay Tug Services. He did not call the U.S. Coast Guard because their base at Grand Marais had closed on September 30. Grand Portage was now in the Duluth Coast Guard jurisdiction, some 46 nautical miles away.[25] Thunder Bay was the closest at 25 nautical miles away.

By now, it was about 10 o'clock in the morning, Eastern Daylight Saving Time. The *Glenada*, regarded as the best ship for the rescue, could not assist. Because the storm was wild enough to warrant moving lakers as well as salties, both tug companies were committed. According to Dana, the Canadian Coast Guard was reluctant to assist because the drifting ship was in American waters. Sharon Dawson, who had been called by both Judith Melby and Dana Kollars, said she notified the Canadian Coast Guard about 11 a.m.

"1630Z—Thunder Bay MCTS Centre becomes aware of the incident when a call from the Westfort (SAR) Base to one of its mobile units is monitored Ch82 indicating that a call was received from the Grampa Woo."[26]

1630Z is Zulu Time used exclusively by the Coast Guard. In Thunder Bay, 1630Z means 11:30 a.m., Eastern Standard Time.

Keck Melby, after being contacted by Dana, was attempting to launch his twenty-six foot boat. Dana said he radioed back and told Keck to forget it, the *Grampa Woo* was so far out it would be dangerous for the small craft to leave the protection of the harbour.

If only the 65 foot ferry, the *Voyageur 11*, had been delayed in its trip to winter dockage in Duluth. According to Dana, it had passed by just a half-hour earlier, only to duck into Grand Marais for shelter from the storm.

Unexpectedly, Dana received an uncanny call from his wife. In a mysterious act of clairvoyance, ChunAe tried to reach the *Grampa Woo*, even though she knew its cellular phone could not receive calls in the enclosure of Grand Portage harbour. When Dana answered she knew the ship without propellers, was adrift in the open Lake, where cellular phone contact was possible.

"He was very calm. I think it has a lot to do with— he's very experienced—he was in the military for twenty years—he's been training soldiers and the tougher a situation gets, the more calm he gets. And he can think straight. But, just by listening to his voice, I know that something is there."[27]

ChunAe got in the car and drove to Grand Portage. She wanted to be near, just in case he needed her help. What that might be, she did not know.

Outside the Grand Portage harbour, and still somewhat in the lee of the west shore, the full fury of the Lake was ahead of them, the west wind blowing them away from the protection of the land. Suddenly, looming through the grey turmoil of the Lake, was a ghostly, giant thousand foot lake freighter, the *Walter J. McCarthy Jr.*

Dana radioed and he radioed.

> "He [Kollars] could see us, but we couldn't see him when he first called. He was too close to shore. We had to wait until he drifted out a bit before we could get close to him."[28]

The *McCarthy,* downbound with 68,194 net tons of coal and with a draw of only 28 feet, could not possibly enter the small harbour of Grand Portage, *Grampa Woo* in tow or not. Thunder Bay harbour, 25 nautical miles to the north, would have to do. The 14,000 horse power *McCarthy* changed course and waited for the *Grampa Woo* to drift out to it. The freighter dropped a line in the water and circled once. The line was too far away. It circled again, and in an incredibly precise manoeuvre for the elephant ship that takes "more than two miles to stop,"[29] it eased up to the *Grampa Woo,* one tenth its size.

> "You don't turn tight circles in a thousand footer, and you don't just stop it. I was worried they'd get blown into us and then pulled under and I'd end up killing the people I was trying to rescue. Our crew was running around on icy decks, in what was eight-foot seas and building. I'm proud of the crew, they did a hell of a job…That boat [*Grampa Woo*] was rocking like a bucking horse."[30]

According to Dana, Captain Smyth asked Dana and Robin to jump aboard, but Dana wanted the *Grampa Woo* taken in tow first. Eventually a three inch towline, thrown to *Grampa Woo*, was able to be affixed to a bridle.

"It was inch and a quarter poly line that was double. It was passed around through the three inch towline and then doubled back and hooked back to the post on the deck."[31]

By then, it was too late to jump to the *McCarthy*.

"Once actually, when the bridle was secure, we were in the bow and the hatch was open and they said jump and Dana actually got onto the railing ready to jump and the boat's going up and down eighteen feet and it's like a huge scissors and they yelled: 'No. No, don't.' I went to grab him and I looked at him and he looked at me and he got back. Ya, he'd have been cut in half. Both of us would have, if we'd have tried."[32]

"It was too dangerous, the back end of our boat was past the stern of the *McCarthy* and it was much more violent and the *Woo* was taking damage from the side of the *McCarthy*."[33]

"By the time we got the towline hooked to our bridle, we had drifted far enough astern to the *McCarthy's* stern that the seas were causing the *Grampa Woo* to pitch and to pitch violently enough that the crew of the *McCarthy* told us not to try and board her at that time."[34]

Once under tow, Dana and Robin went inside the relatively stabilized *Grampa Woo*, where it was warm and dry because the engines were running. They huddled in sleeping bags until warmed up. Dana actually went to sleep for a while.

Robin went up to the wheelhouse. He noted how far from shore they were.

"If he could have got closer, there would have been much less fetch and a lot less risk for us. And that was punctuated by another ship—and I've forgotten the name *[Oglebay Norton]* cruising along the inside. I asked Dana: 'Don't you want to say anything?' And he said, 'No. I don't want to create any bad feelings. The guy's already PO'd at us, so let's not make it worse by trying to tell him how to do his job.'"[35]

Thunder Bay Tug Services and the Coast Guard were contacted by Dana again. He asked for a tug to meet them at the entrance to greater Thunder Bay harbour to take over the tow from the *McCarthy* and get them safely to dockage. By then, Gerry Dawson on the *Glenada* had finished his commitment to the lake freighters. He accepted what he thought was a routine job, departing Keefer Terminal at 4:52 p.m. The *Glenada* hid in the lee of Turtlehead while waiting to rendez-vous with *Grampa Woo*. The Coast Guard vessel *Westfort* was tasked to accompany them.

Everyone knew that, if the towline was going to break, it would break as the *McCarthy* veered away from its northeasterly heading to make the turn west towards Thunder Bay harbour. Not only the pressure of the turn but the full force of the north-west wind would increase the strain on the towline. Dana was worried about the damage the bridle had sustained as the *Woo* rubbed along the side of the *McCarthy*. His worries were well founded. The bridle did snap.

"Sure enough, when we made that turn, the line did break and funnily enough, we were both on the bridge. Dana was actually watching the line as it broke. And that was kind of freaky."[36]

The *McCarthy* was having its own problems.

"It was a maelstrom of wind and waves at the mouth. Our anemometer was reading 60 knots [about seventy miles per hour] winds at that point, and the seas were all of 15 feet or more. We were rolling like a pig, and that little boat was really bouncing around. That's when their part of the bridle parted."[37]

Everyone's worst fears were confirmed.

The *McCarthy* and the *Oglebay Norton* continued on. The *Grampa Woo* turned its hope towards the *Glenada*.

"We knew there was a salvage tug that was waiting for us inside. We didn't know if they would attempt to make it outside. We pretty much presumed they wouldn't. Or I had."[38]

7 ~ THE LONGEST HOUR

It is all in being ready.

When they saw the Christmas tree lights of the *McCarthy* prick through the squalling snow, without hesitation the *Westfort* and *Glenada* left the shelter of Turtlehead on the north-east tip of Pie Island, the southern portal of the greater harbour of Thunder Bay. They had been waiting for more than half an hour. The two little ships headed out towards the notorious Thunder Cape, the northern portal of the greater harbour, into the roaring black of the open water of the shipping channel.

As pre-arranged, the *Glenada* would take over the tow of the *Grampa Woo*.

"As darkness fell, so did the temperature. Winds building to 60 knots were rapidly driving the waves to 12 to 18 feet. Wind-driven spray froze instantly to the decks and superstructure of the vessels. If only the towline had held."[1]

It did not. When the *McCarthy* made the turn from its position north-east of Angus Island, just off the protruding headland of Turtlehead, the bridle holding the towline parted. Snapped. It was now the full black of seven o'clock.

Chief Coxswain Bob King on the *Westfort* felt they were in "the worst possible spot you could get on the Lake at that particular time."[2]

Others would agree.

"At Thunder Cape, at the foot of the Sleeping Giant, a lot of Lake captains say that they'd rather sail anywhere in the world than around that Cape."[3]

"They say they fear that more than any place else they've sailed in the world. They say you never know what you're going to get when you round it. There haven't been that many sinkings out there. No. What happens is they know once they get beyond that, there's no turning around, so a lot of them will go out there, take a look, if they see heavy seas out there, they'll turn around and come back to shelter."[4]

"It is not uncommon to have the wind coming from two different directions at the same time, and it makes a really boiling cauldron of waves every which way."[5]

"During a recent trip of a 730 foot lake freighter, four people had to be taken to the hospital. The waves at Thunder Cape had knocked three of them out of their bunk, and knocked apart the bed of the other."[6]

No longer buffered by islands, a north-west wind can funnel directly across the fetch of the greater harbour. The wind can also hit the enormous north-south body of the

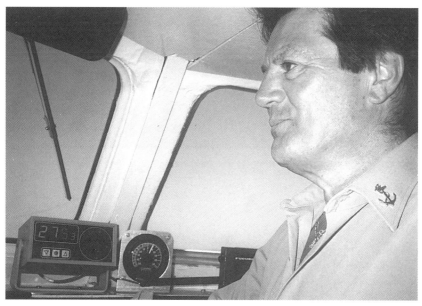

Bob King, Chief Coxswain of *CCGC Westfort.*

Sleeping Giant at the foot of the 32 mile Sibley Peninsula,[7] veering southward along both its sides. On October 30, "three different wave patterns"[8] were created. Even worse, Bob King thought the wind would be "hitting the towline dead on and if that rope was going to break, we all knew that it would break there, or at least I did."[9]

"I talked to the captain of the *McCarthy* and he had everybody up on the ship. All hands were called to station, and he said that his ship was rolling like a pig and he didn't sound too...He wasn't really happy at all. They don't like to be out in that kind of weather."[10]

When the towing apparatus parted, the two rescuing ships had to chase after the *Grampa Woo*, "a mile and-a-half away."[11] Drifting sideways at a speed of 3.5 to 4 knots, it was moving at a good walking pace.

"It was not like they were waiting for somebody."[12]

Captain Dawson could sense the tension in Dana Kollar's voice over the radio, as he exclaimed, "You had better hurry."[13]

With disappointment, Gerry Dawson heard the radio transmission from the *McCarthy*.

"The captain of the *McCarthy* then told his crew to haul in their towline and he told the crew of the *Grampa Woo*, quote, 'You better get that tug and Coast Guard Cutter out here!' That was the last radio communication we had with the only other vessel that could have provided assistance or support to the tug *Glenada*, CCGC *Westfort*, or the *Grampa Woo*."[14]

Terse conversations were going on between the ships and between the Coast Guard centres, one in Duluth, one in Thunder Bay, and one at the Central and Arctic Regional command centre in Trenton, Ontario. Some calls were by radio, some by phone. Not all channels were available to everyone and information had to be relayed.

"It's like a circus there. You've got three or four people talking to you. The phones are ringing."[15]

When hearing the *McCarthy* broadcast, Gerry was slapped with a sudden realization. He could not count on the thousand foot hulk of the *McCarthy* to provide a lee to calm the waters and facilitate the establishing of another towline.

The *Glenada* would have to do it alone. When he caught up to the *Grampa Woo,* and manoeuvred the tug closer, he could not help but be impressed with the ship.

"I had my first view of the luxurious craft, illuminated with our searchlight on the outside, and glowing internally from her own power. I could see the two men scrambling about, one in the blue pilot house on the upper deck, and the second man, on the bow trying to gain a footing in the treacherous conditions."[16]

Now two and-a-half miles off Trowbridge Island and more than half the way across the entrance to the harbour, the *Glenada*, alongside the *Woo*, kept trying for more than an hour to secure a line to it.

"Jim Harding on our tug deck, dressed in a Stearns Anti-Exposure suit and running shoes, was being tested by every wave as the decks grew iced over and extremely treacherous. I tried to get close to the *Woo* by heading at it, but we were tossed by the seas in different directions. Jim informed me that our towline and bridle were now frozen to the stern tow bitts, and were going to be difficult to use. I didn't realize until later that for the majority of the time, he was just able to hold onto the tow bitts while his legs were floating out behind him because our stern deck was completely underwater.

"In the wheelhouse, as I tried to back into the seas to get a better angle of approach, the waves would crash into our stern, lifting it, and tossing spray well forward and over the wheelhouse. I tried again to get to the *Woo*, but the waves pushed us to port and surged us forward as I got close to their line. I was afraid we would suck their towline into our propeller or get tossed on top of the *Woo*. Once again, I attempted to get close, and this time, Jim was able to grab their trailing line, a small half-inch poly rope, and tie it to our shoulder bitts. We both knew it wouldn't be strong enough to tow them with the two storey waves and storm force winds. He tried to go aft for our four inch towline, as I tried to keep the tug close enough to keep the tension off the line. Before Jim could move five feet on the slippery, ice-covered decks, the line parted.

"We backed away taking spray and water over our decks, completely engulfing Jim. I manoeuvred the tug around the stern of the *Grampa Woo* and tried a different angle of approach, but again the seas would not allow us the chance to get our line aboard the *Woo*. My wheelhouse window became iced over from the freezing spray and my visibility was reduced to an area the size of an envelope in only one window."[17]

The *Westfort*, trying to maintain a steady position in relationship to the *Glenada* and the *Grampa Woo*, had one person on the radio, one person spotting waves out the back and another on the wheel.

"With the wind and the ice, you couldn't see. That's what made it all the more dangerous. It's like looking through a coke bottle from the bottom. In the daytime, you have a fighting chance but at night-time, you've got to be lucky. We couldn't even see the Trowbridge Lighthouse and that thing is 100 feet above water. We'd only see it occasionally."[18]

"Our whole superstructure was just encased in ice and we couldn't see at all. All we could see is lights from Dawson's tug. Sometimes you could see two separate lights and it looked eerie because, with the ice encrusted on the windows, you could just see weird lights. It looked kind of like an alien thing, and you're

Lake Superior wave.

pitching and tossing so much, and sometimes you're under water and you see weird. It was a horrible, horrible situation. It was just awful."[19]

The *Westfort* realized it was taking on water in its buoyancy chambers. Instead of the flotation effect for which they were designed, the chambers were exerting a downward pressure. The vessel was becoming sluggish and unresponsive.

"At 7:40 p.m., the *Westfort* called from half-mile away, and said they were taking on water, icing up badly, and didn't know how much longer they could take it. All of a sudden, Bob King's next words from the *Westfort* were, 'We're going over,' and then the radio was quiet."[20]

Gerry did not have the reassurance of hearing crewperson Inga Thorsteinson shout over the noise of the engine and the storm, "No we're NOT."[21] She admits she said it because she simply could not accept the possibility.

"At the same time as the *Westfort* disappeared, I had lost communication with Jim, and my worst fear was that he had been washed overboard."[22]

Inga Thorsteinson could not acccept the possibility of the *Westfort* going over.

"As captain, it's your worst fear, someone goin' over the side."[23]

Gerry turned the tug away from *Grampa Woo* to look for his man. The waves were now 15 to 20 feet.

"I started to head back into the sea as much as I could, up towards the west, back towards town just to give myself a few seconds so that I could look out the windows. I ran from one window to the other and then shouted into the intercom. Finally he tapped on the window and I knew he was all right."[24]

"The lyrics of Gordon Lightfoot's song were playing over and over in my mind, 'Where does the love of God go, when the waves turn the minutes to hours,' well it seemed like 'days' before I heard the tap of a pike pole at the side window and realized I still had Jim with me.

I called him inside, meanwhile checking the radar screen for the missing green dot as well as looking visually for the familiar red and yellow hull of the *Westfort*. I was unable to locate them.

I sent Jim below to check on Jack in the engine room and to check and see how things were surviving in the galley."[25]

Although the leadership of the rescue was Gerry Dawson's sole responsibility, he felt he was never alone. Even when he thought Jim might have gone overboard and the *Westfort* might have sunk, and technically he may have been alone, he knew he was not. He had an almost tele-pathic feeling that Jim would not desert him. As well, there was other mental energy around him as he sat on his solitudinous perch in the wheelhouse.

"My Dad, every time I go out on the boat I think he's with me. I just knew he was there watching over me *that night* and he's there quite often with me."[26]

Gerry felt there was another being there with him, too.

"I'm not a strong religious person, but I do believe in a superior being and I do pray to Him quite often when I'm out on the boat to get me through certain cir-cumstances and things like that."[27]

When Jim returned from checking on Jack in the engine room, it was unwelcome information he bore.

"Jim returned with the news that Jack had been overcome by fuel oil fumes and lay ill in his bunk. Jack had stayed diligently in the engine room to ensure that our engines would not let us down. The fact that we had been delivered some watery fuel a few weeks previous had played heavily on both our minds. If the water was going to surface, the agitation from the rolling seas would certainly bring it up from the bottom of our tanks."[28]

If water got in the engine, it would stall, like cholesterol sabotaging a heart. Without "The Heart" as the crew called the engine, the *Glenada* would be unable to manoeuvre and maintain its stability. Broadside—sideways—in the waves, it was no match for the dispassionate force of the sea. It would broach and roll over.

Despite the frenzied churning of sound outside, Gerry did not hear it. He only was listening for the throb of the engine. Jim would not remember any sound. He was too busy watching for whatever waves he could see in the dark.

Half of his worries relieved by Jim's reappearance, Gerry still could not see the *Westfort* on the radar. Should he begin a search for its survivors, if any? And what about the engineerless engine room?

"The *Westfort* finally radioed back that they were holding their own, but being tossed violently by the seas and rolling up to 80 degrees from side to side. I could barely see them, as they were disappearing into the trough of the waves and our radar was unable to discriminate between their craft and the crests of the waves. It was at this point that I decided we had better forget about trying to save the *Grampa Woo* and concentrate on saving her crew. I radioed Chief Coxswain Bob King on the *Westfort* about the possibility of them rescuing the two men, as their vessel, with two engines, was more manoeuvrable. Bob informed me they would not be able to get close enough to remove the men without sustaining major damage to both vessels."[29]

Tipping from rail to rail, the *Westfort* was continuing to take on water in the void space designed to maintain buoyancy. The feet of the crew were leaving the deck with the bunt of each unseen wave, their voices hoarse from thirst and yelling to each other. The communication head-phones were unuseable because of possible entanglement with crew members as they moved about frantically in the claustrophobic wheelhouse. In addition to the unresponsiveness of the ship, visibility was virtually nil through the windows. The superstructure had iced up.

"It wasn't the darkness that bothered us and it wasn't the waves. It was the ice."[30]

When the Rescue Coordination Centre in Trenton learned of the *Westfort's* condition through the Marine Communications and Traffic Services in Thunder Bay, the Trenton base asked for the *Westfort's* position. However, their longitude and latitude were virtually impossible to establish. Their ingenuity was being taxed just to keep the ship stable. The punching of the waves was knocking them into the air. Exertion and stress made them breathless, sick and dehydrated. When Thunder Bay MCTS again informed Trenton of the *Westfort's* dire plight, this time the base said the rescue vessel could break off and seek shelter.

It did not. The *Westfort* maintained its position on scene. In addition, Bob King asked that a helicopter be sent to pick the men off the *Grampa Woo*. The closest chopper was in Traverse City, more than a hundred miles away on Lake Michigan. With no "Estimated Time of Arrival," at least the helicopter plan was an alternative. Options had all but disappeared. The *Glenada* could not get a towline to the *Grampa Woo* and certainly there were no other ships in the area that could or would help.

The U.S. Coast Guard in Duluth was being kept informed by Thunder Bay. They too had been thinking about possible assistance from the *McCarthy,* but had been unable to make radio contact.

"My Group were thinking if she could put them in her lee...if she could put them in her shadow...she casts a helluva shadow."[31]

Bob King did not think it was feasible. The *McCarthy* had played its part by dragging *Grampa Woo* into a location where Thunder Bay vessels could assist it. Besides, the men on the *Grampa Woo* were considering abandoning ship.

Dana and Gerry, although in different ships, and without discussion, seemed to arrive at the same conclusion. The only option left was to abandon ship. Neither knew about a possible rescue by helicopter, an exercise that would want the men to stay aboard the *Woo* in order to have as large a pick-up platform as possible.

What else was there to do but abandon ship? The tow-lines were frozen "like steel cables,"[32] and the *Westfort* was barely surviving. The *Woo* was drifting inexorably towards the craggy rocks of Isle Royale, if indeed the ship could stay upright that long, and if the men could survive the cold and exhausting buffeting for another two hours or so.

"I suggested to Dana that he could consider abandoning their vessel and boarding their life raft. As difficult a decision as it was, he seemed to realize that he had no choice."[33]

Although Robin was not exactly happy about getting into the raft, he collected up his chief's documents and papers and put them in a fanny pack for him. All Robin grabbed for himself was a teddy bear that had a special meaning for him. He stuffed it inside the top of his wet suit.

For Robin, the thought of getting into the "fishnet" life raft with his backside exposed to the frigid waters of the Lake was his second moment of greatest despair. Even the rocks of Isle Royale were more appealing. But not for Dana.

"It's a conscious decision. It wasn't a matter of panic: let's get the hell off this boat. It was a conscious decision. We were exhausted, no more resources, no more lines that weren't frozen to the deck."[34]

As yet not aware of the inadequacies of the life-saving equipment, however legal, Gerry's plan was to have Dana and Robin, once in a life raft, float a trailing line to the

Glenada. Jim would pick it up and the life raft would be towed to port.

"Something in the back of my mind made me ask him if the life raft had a cover, and his reply was, 'No, and it doesn't have a bottom either!' I again brought the tug close enough to see their raft and when I shone my searchlight at the boat and saw a rectangular ring float with a mesh bottom and two men in wet suits, one with only the top; I told them to forget the life raft idea. I checked my radar and realized we were now six miles from the closest land, in 20 foot seas and 70 knot winds with freezing temperatures, and felt that jumping into an open life raft of this nature would be utter suicide. If the cold waves didn't kill them, I felt that as soon as we took up tension on the line to tow them, the line would have snapped the raft in pieces."[35]

Flung into Lake Superior, how long would a person last?

"Optimum conditions on a nice summer day and calm, maybe 45 minutes. But that night that we were out, gee whiz, you wouldn't last five minutes."[36]

Learning about the helicopter, Gerry realized it could be hours before it arrived, if indeed with the storm it could arrive. He realized the difficulty of plucking two men from the bouncing deck of a wallowing ship, if indeed the wallowing *Grampa Woo* would remain upright until the helicopter arrived, considering the top-heavy weight of the freezing spray coating all the ships. Dana and Robin simply might not survive the wait. Gerry, in consultation with Jim, then advised a last desperate plan.

"There was other lives at stake so you have to sort of expand where you're going to draw the line. For people, ya."[37]

Gerry radioed the men on *Grampa Woo*. He said he would bring the *Glenada* in close and they should be prepared to board the tug. Gerry knew the dangers. One hundred and fifty feet of rope snaking out behind *Grampa Woo* threatened to deaden the *Glenada's* engines, perhaps even coil the two ships together, bashing them against each other as both ships floated dead in the water towards Isle Royale. Perhaps, the low bow of the *Glenada* would punch a hole in the hull or bottom of *Grampa Woo* and the ship would sink. Or someone could get mangled by the scissoring action of the ships as earlier feared with the *McCarthy*.

"For the *Glenada*, it was a tail sea, a stern sea; for *Grampa Woo* it was a beam sea."[38]

"I would get as close as I could and have Jim try to help them aboard. I came up to within ten feet of the stern on the starboard quarter, bumped the *Woo*, crushing a part of the white hand railing, and then backed off before I did too much damage, or hurt anyone. I made a second attempt, putting my bow perpendicular to his stern, just a foot or so away, [just past the starboard corner] with our large black tires providing a fender between us. I couldn't see much, as my wheelhouse windows were still coated in ice, but I could see Jim grabbing one man and then the other and pulling them aboard the tug."[39]

"I don't know whether the wind died or what. I can't even remember what happened at that point but it just seemed to lay down enough."[40]

Jim remembers:

"Dana got his hands on the tire. He just kind of reached down. I grabbed him by the butt and threw him on the deck and basically said, you know, 'Don't even try to stand up.' "[41]

"Once Jim signalled that they were safely aboard, I backed away, still aware that the trailing line from the *Woo* was extremely close to our propeller. I radioed the *Westfort* with the words, 'We've got them.' "[42]

Unlike the scissoring action of the side-by-side *Grampa Woo* and the *McCarthy*, back the eternity of some four hours ago when Dana and Robin faced the real possibility of being cut in half if they jumped from one ship to the other, the *Grampa Woo* and the *Glenada* remained on the same plane for an instant. Gerry somehow was able to bring the two ships level with each other even though the waves were now more than twice the size. With the split second timing of an athlete—"the job keeps me in shape"[43]—Jim was able to grab Dana, then Robin, and pull them off the lurching ship.

Was it luck? Or incredible dexterity on Gerry's part to nose the big kissing tire on the bow of the *Glenada* up to the rear end of the wallowing *Woo* at precisely the right moment? Was it Jim's courage and physical ability?

Or was it one of those mysterious Lake Superior lulls when the erratic waves hit a momentary calm? Men and the Lake working together? If it was a lull—a window— Gerry saw his opportunity and acted. Jim reacted. Dana and Robin reacted. They were aboard the *Glenada*! They crawled over the wet, icy deck that was "like a curling rink,"[44] through a wall of water whooshing down on them, and into the cabin and warmth. They had been on the propellerless *Grampa Woo* for 12 hours.

"We now had no choice but to leave the *Grampa Woo* drifting at the mercy of a Superior storm. It was an eerie feeling and extremely difficult for me to watch this beautiful yacht ablaze with lights, bob away like a ghost ship on the waves. I will never forget my feelings of helplessness and disappointment at not being able to save her. As well, I was haunted by the uncertainty of what would be her fate."[45]

According to Canadian Coast Guard records, it had taken one hour and fifteen minutes for the two ships to catch the drifting *Woo*, attempt to get it in tow, back away and regroup, and finally zero in and grab the men off. For those involved, it seemed much longer. The minutes, as in Gordon Lightfoot's song, had turned to hours. Gerry said, "Days."

The beleaguered flotilla, now only two ships, headed towards Tee Harbour, a haven of refuge shaped like a tee at the foot of the Sleeping Giant. Empty and without guidance, direction or purpose, *Grampa Woo* lurched out to sea.

On the airwaves:

> "The Westfort just told me that the Grenada (sic) got two men off. You can cancel the chopper. Just heading into a local harbour to wait out the storm and the tug Grenada with the two men on board is heading back. The Grampa Woo is two-and-a-half miles off of Trowbridge and is abandoned and drifting."

> "Okay."
> "So."
> "Ya."
> "A turn for the luck."[46]

The 'long and lat' of the drifting *Grampa Woo* was established to be N 48: 13:74 W 89:95 18 and a 'notship'—a notice to shipping—was issued.

But the drama and difficulty were not yet over. The wind had not abated. The icing and the lack of visibility for both ships were increasing. The *Westfort* was still sluggish because of loss of buoyancy. Earlier the *Glenada* had realized it must head for the shelter of Tee Harbour, with or without *Grampa Woo*. The *Westfort* agreed. To get there, they had to fight their way across six more miles of seething sea.

> "We were getting pounded sideways and from the bow, and about every third wave or fourth wave you'd get it broadside. It cleared everything in the wheelhouse. Everything was just cleared right out. My little heater, I had it up there a few times trying to get the ice off the window. Everything was just a mess inside. The wind and the waves were knocking us all over."[47]

As they approached the eastward side of the Sleeping Giant, all crews anticipated a respite from the winds. Inexplicably, there was none.

"It was twisting around the Cape and coming from two different directions in ferocious gusts. I guess it was making a vortex."[48]

The short range scale of the radar of the *Glenada* had gone out because of the freezing spray. Out of necessity it was following the *Westfort* into Tee Harbour.

"We were travelling pretty close together anyways so, when I got around the corner, it was wild again, we couldn't see anything, furious winds, 70 knot winds, blowing like crazy, so I eased off on the throttle and was just trying to take a look around and see where the hell we were going to go and where Gerry and the rest of them went. I saw the radar screen going around like that and I'm momentarily confused. The ship got caught in the wind and we were blowing out to the rocks. So we were in trouble again."[49]

Within a hundred feet of the supposed shelter, spotlights scanning the shore, white spray leaping above the black rocks, the wind just took the little ship and flung it around in a complete circle. A spiral. Some say it was flung around more than once. The radar went crazy.

"Anyways, we had to kick the window open. We got the window open and I had to stick my head out the window and face the wind and run that boat with the window open. I guess the wind was coming up over the cliffs, doing funny things coming around Thunder Cape. It was catatonic."[50]

In the whole situation, the ship going over rail to rail, the blindness of the night, the icing up, and the sluggishness, it was the wind picking up their vessel and flinging it around in a circle, or circles, that made Inga sit up and take notice.

"That was when I was pretty nervous. That's when it struck home to me just how powerful that wind was. It was so strong that even with the engines full ahead and the rudders hard over, we couldn't turn up into it."[51]

The *Westfort* actually ended up facing out of the harbour and heading straight towards the *Glenada*.[52]

Gerry shone his searchlight at the *Westfort* to help the crew orient itself. He radioed to say he was going to beach the tug for the night. Eventually the *Westfort* was able to turn up into the wind and make its way, rafting up to the *Glenada* on shore beside an old 'fish dock.'

For the first time, they heard the sound of the storm—"Roaring"[53]—previously obscured by engine noise and their attention to the job and survival. No one heard the wind or the waves during the whole event; even though beached, the vessels fought the wind with their engines running and the wheel hard over. Inga and Gerry stayed in their respective wheelhouses.

It was 8:57 p.m., more than two hours after the towline parted and the *Glenada* and the *Westfort* left the shelter of Turtlehead. More than two hours of being whipped by hurricane force winds and in seas all the ships, even thousand foot lake freighters, would rather avoid.

The *Glenada* leaving Thunder Cape on the third day after the rescue.

8 ~ AFTERWARDS

The blight of futility that lies in wait for men's speeches had fallen upon our conversation, and made it a thing of empty sounds.

It may have been anger, maybe guilt, maybe just plain exhaustion, but the two Captains, the rescued and the rescuer, did not meet after the *Glenada* landed in the relative safety of Tee Harbour. There was no conquering hero party or jubilant celebration, maybe some jokes in the wheelhouse about the propriety of taking all the propellers off a ship when the replacements were still en route, Jack Olson always ready with a good-natured jibe, no matter how tired.

"We hounded him unmercifully for not having propellers on the boat."[1]

Gerry jibed Jack about his sickness during the storm by saying it was lucky Jack had cooked a good dinner on the way over because he had to taste it twice.

The crew went about cleaning up the mess in the wheelhouse, galley and engine room. Everything that was unbolted had been flung about. Both crews began the lengthy task of chipping the ice off the ships. Gerry stayed up in the wheelhouse, monitoring the engines that were kept running in order to keep the ship nosed into the sand. He was nursing an anger at the lives which he felt had been placed in needless jeopardy. He was nursing a guilt about his own inability to save the beautiful *Grampa Woo*. He was nursing a resentment that the *McCarthy* had sought shelter while three ships a tenth its size or less, struggled in towering seas.

Gerry's adrenalized state continued. His heart pounded. His hands shook. He even smoked some cigarettes, not his special cigarillos. He could not sleep. Jim and Willie came up and sat with him—but the image of the *Grampa Woo* kept flashing into his mind.

"All I could see was that magnificent white and blue hull drifting out of my reach and off to the east."[2]

"It just kept going through the back of my mind what I could have done, what I should have done, different things."[3]

Dana crawled into a bunk, utterly spent, his easy loquaciousness and charm gone. He and Robin had been up since four o'clock that morning, much of that time being flung from side to side by the punishing behaviour of *Grampa Woo*.

Bob King had pains in his stomach like an appendix attack.

"I'm sure Bob King was pretty rattled about the whole thing and I don't blame him. They were in a lot smaller boat than we were and they were getting pushed around pretty good."[4]

"We learned later that the *Westfort* engines have a mercury switch that kills the engines if they roll over ninety degrees. Ten more degrees in the seas, and we would have had two helpless vessels to attempt to save."[5]

It is called the zero-moment point, the point of no return.

"The capsize switch is a tube filled with mercury and at a certain angle the mercury sloshes up and contact is lost and the engines shut off."[6]

"It was real dramatic, almost thought we were going to lose a few men (sic)."[7]

Inga, whose turn it was to be engineer of the *Westfort*, stayed with the ship and monitored the engines, kept running in case the wind tried to have its way again.

"That night after we got in, I don't think our stomachs were settled enough to eat anything. I think we just gathered for coffee that first night after we tied up."[8]

After sitting in the galley for a few minutes, Robin went up to the wheelhouse and thanked Gerry.

Jack, knowing Gerry and Jim were watching the gauges, slept.

"I don't lose much sleep over much anyway."[9]

Not Willie.

"I don't think I slept for three days. I may have slept the second night a little bit."[10]

From the routine trip that was to take a couple of hours, the crews did not return until the third day.

"On the second day, I went to check it out and there were hundreds of these water spouts like mini-tornadoes

Rescuing people from the breakwall and stalled boats is routine. The rescue of October 30, 1996, at the foot of the notorious Thunder Cape, is remembered as *that night*, not routine at all. The rescuer, Captain Gerry Dawson, and the rescued, Captain Dana Kollars and crewman Robin Sivill, smile when they return safely to port after a 3-day saga.

a hundred feet high just dancing like ballerinas across the water outside Tee Harbour. It was wild."[11]

"We started getting a little bit hummy after while."[12]

Inga had been trying out a brand new dry suit.

"It was a watertight dry suit with a gasket around the neck and the wrists, and it was beautiful and warm, and when I took it off, I had sort of felt coveralls on. They were grey felt coveralls. They were like wearing pyjamas. It would have saved my life if I went overboard because it was water tight and insulated, but it allowed me to work. I didn't feel like wearing a full suit which almost looks like a diver's suit, so Jack kindly lend me a pair of his workboots, so you could see me clumping around the deck of the *Westfort* knocking the ice off the railings with this funny grey suit and these big workboots. Quite a sight. "[13]

Although the *Glenada* was well stocked with food, the *Westfort* had nothing but emergency rations. A Coast Guard helicopter dropped food, some clothes, and cigarettes.

"Willie requesting that, if possible, Coast Guard chopper bring out a couple packs of cigarettes, Du Maurier light regular and Export A light regular."[14]

With no shortage of cigarettes, or food, Jack was in his element in the galley cooking up meals for everyone.

"We had pork chops, mushroom sauce and mashed potatoes, but I'm cooking for eight guys (sic) on a hot plate for Christ's sake and an electric frying pan."[15]

"The cholesterol level!"[16]

The crews continued chipping the lacquered ice from their ships. The *Westfort* crew moved their deck box off onto the *Glenada* and pumped out the void space, trying to make the ship as stable as possible for its return. Gerry checked out his tug. Only the microwave was damaged.

At about 10 a.m., Dana climbed the long climb of gratitude up to the wheelhouse. The two men whose lives had become so indelibly entwined finally met. Dana introduced himself and thanked Gerry.

Gerry was unnerved by Dana's calm. He later learned of Dana's other harrowing near-death experiences which had made him cool in the face of disaster. Jim observed that both Dana and Robin were "remarkably mentally whole."[17]

Dana's aplomb broke, however, when he learned by radio that the U.S. Coast Guard had done a flyover and found *Grampa Woo* lying low in the water, alongside Passage Island north east of the tip of Isle Royale. A sleek, white carcass impaled on rocks that had gutted it like a filleting knife, the sea had washed it free of its grizzles of ice. It was Dana's second moment of great despair. He had hoped against hope that *Grampa Woo* would miss the islands and rocks at the entrance to Thunder Bay greater harbour and glide out into the open Lake. There they could catch it the next day, if the weather settled, which it did not.

"Wrecked right below Passage Island Light and literally hit a rock face, the last piece of rock between there and Sault Ste. Marie, three hundred or so miles

Wave action pivoted *Grampa Woo* around on the impaling rocks.

away. If it had missed that rock, it would have gone and gone and gone and probably would have been salvaged."[18]

"That's when he broke down when he heard that his boat was wrecked."[19]

Dana later learned the ship's fate in detail.

"The damage was phenomenal. She was ripped apart even though she looked intact. She had huge cracks all the way around the midship down into the water. Robin boarded her and saw huge bounders protruding through her hull up into the passenger area, up into the galley, and the engine was completely ripped out. She was a total loss and yet she was still above water."[20]

Lifejackets and miscellany from the ship were flung onto rocks and wedged into cracks twenty feet high.

"So if they had stayed with the boat, I think that's where they would have ended up, somewhere up there."[21]

Later, the wind pivoted *Grampa Woo* around on the impaling rocks, the stern riding high up the cliff, the luxury wheelhouse tilted into total submersion in the water, the engine excised and thrown away to its own open grave.

The wreck was no match for Lake Superior. By August, ten months later, Alexander Paterson, who dived the *Grampa Woo* wreck with Don Price of Winnipeg, as well as the nearby *America* and the *Emperor*, said the damage was continuing.

"The boat was completely gone below the water line. It's like somebody cut it with a can opener. There's no question it's dangerous. There's a lot of really sharp aluminum. This thing was torn up like someone shredded a piece of paper. The whole shore is covered with garbage, it doesn't look like anything else but garbage, little bits of pieces of life jackets and rope and torn pieces of plastic."[22]

Divers, Alexander Paterson of Thunder Bay, and Don Price of Winnipeg, have explored the remains of *Grampa Woo*.

After the despair of learning of the ship's fate, Dana rallied quickly. His enthusiastic verve returned. With his usual aplomb, he fielded questions from the multi-media which began to bombard not only him, but Gerry and Bob on the radio phone.

Richard Boone of CJLB Country Music Station in Thunder Bay had been checking weather stations and the police about the storm which the city felt was tormenting it. Acting on an astute hunch, he just happened to call the Coast Guard base and learned about the drama in progress, a thousand foot laker trying to tow a luxury cruise ship to safety. All media jumped on the story. The harbourfront city of Thunder Bay adopted the drama as its own. It was media delight. Would the towline from the *McCarthy* break? No. But the bridle did. Would the *Glenada* get *Grampa Woo*? No. Could the little ships weather the storm? Yes. Could the *Glenada* get the men? Yes. Would *Grampa Woo* miss the rocks? No. Could the other ships return to Thunder Bay? No. When?

Gerry's mother learned of the drama just as the *Glenada* was docking.

When the ships finally arrived in port three days later at about 1:30 p.m. Friday, family, friends and, of course, the media were there. ChunAe, who had driven to Thunder Bay, wanted to spirit Dana away to spare him questioning by the media. But Dana had recovered. He was in his element.

"Adventure? I don't have my dictionary with me, but odyssey, I believe would be another term...In between the period of removing the old propellers and putting on the new propellers, 60 knot winds in the Bay of Grand Portage began pushing the *Grampa Woo* out to sea, pulling her 3,000 pound steel mooring with her...There were some nasty seas out there and I'm sure Gerry was sitting in the *Glenada* with his fingers crossed, hoping that we'd get a lot closer than we did...I was really pleased when Gerry came on the radio and said he was coming and he could probably hear the begging in my voice...Gerry brought that boat in so well that we just did a little six inch hop to get on board...I found out that Gerry's visibility to do all of that was reduced to a little tiny hole through the windshield of the *Glenada*. He used the x-ray vision that all Captains have up in Thunder Bay..."[23]

"They are three of the best mariners I ever met."[24]

"It's nice to be able to take a deep breath...Where's the closet toothbrush?"[25]

"He often quipped it was the first time it ever felt good to have another man grab his butt."[26]

In the car on the way back to their home in Beaver Bay, Minnesota, Dana's bravado left him again. He and ChunAe realized their livelihood and future were now uncertain.

"Our ship was gone. We'd been beaten. People adopt ships as a friend or as a being. So we were, I was, and my wife was also, we were in mourning for losing a member of the family."[27]

Now, after nine years on Lake Superior, he was returning home to Beaver Bay, feeling like a beaten man. Yes, he and crewman, Robin Sivill, had survived a three-day ordeal near the notorious Thunder Cape, for which he was thankful. But he had lost his beloved ship, everything on it, and his source of livelihood. ChunAe sat beside him in the car. In a moment of utter dejection, he wondered out loud if maybe they should return to agriculture and to farming, maybe a chicken ranch. The idea did not last long.

The first step to recovery began when the Kollars arrived home. The people and the communities around Beaver Bay rallied with support, letters, phone-calls, even money. They made him realize his ship was part of the boating heritage of the area, a continuation of the steamships, *America* and *Wenonah*, and the mystique and excitement and business these glamorous ships brought.

"It made us appreciate how much of the community we really are."[28]

How could he leave? How often had he walked across the deck in his hand-swinging military stride, his short dark hair neat and impeccably coiffed, and think, if he did not say it aloud in a voice with a slight southern lilt, "I love my job."

Dana realized if he could, he would stay with boating and Lake Superior. He felt he was not at fault in the combination of circumstances that swept *Grampa Woo* out to sea. The big question was, would his insurance company and the Coast Guard realize it too? Would his name be cleared and his ship replaced?

"Fortunately for us, the U.S. Coast Guard conducted a very thorough investigation and found that our record was spotless and, the insurance company, obviously having to hand over $475,000, would not have done it right away if there was any opportunity to show negligence. The clause in the insurance policy says right there that the Captain must keep the ship in running condition and maintain a certain level of readiness—it is his responsibility—before they make payment and a $475,000 cheque wouldn't be issued immediately if there was any hint of that sort of disregard for the vessel or negligence at all."[29]

"So, just the fact that the insurance company paid right away was very, very comforting to me as the Captain, as a reaffirmation that we did everything with great prudence."[30]

The comments of the U.S. Coast Guard *Marine Casualty Narrative Supplement* also must have been comforting to Dana:

"There is no evidence of actionable misconduct, inattention to duty, negligence, or willful violations of law or regulation on the part of any licensed or certificated personnel, nor evidence of failure of inspected equipment or material, nor evidence that any personnel of the Coast Guard contributed to this casualty."[31]

With the insurance money forthcoming, Dana and ChunAe rallied. They searched around and bought a sister ship of *Grampa Woo*. They called it *Grampa Woo III*, "a better vessel."[32] That it was unlucky to name a boat after one that had sunk was tantamount to worrying about Friday the thirteenth, according to Dana. After all, he was born on Friday the thirteenth and had had his share of luck.

Grampa Woo III is also a Camcraft, manufactured in Crown Point, Louisiana. It was converted in 1986 as a dinner cruise boat, an excursion boat with the cabins added.[33] It has both a dive platform and a fishing platform, but not the extended bowsprit like its predecessor.

There was another considerable change between *Grampa Woo II* and *Grampa Woo III*: better life rafts!

"They have a cover and a top on them."
"And a bottom?"
"Yes."[34]

"In getting this boat, it was outfitted with the same unacceptable life floats and so I made a concerted effort to get these really safe and reliable pieces of

Grampa Woo III moored at Beaver Bay, Minnesota, is a better ship.

These legal mesh-bottom life rafts have been replaced on the *Grampa Woo III*.

lifesaving equipment so I can look into the eyes of my clients and say, 'You know, we're going to take care of you.' It has been pointed out to me last fall that there are times when you can't anticipate those situations."[35]

The Kollars' business the next summer did not suffer. In fact, it was up "sixty percent."[36] Dana is quick to say the increase was not just because of the media attention but also "...because of last year's performance, people rode the boat and told their friends and relatives. But in all honesty, the attention from the media had a positive effect."[37]

Each like a proverbial phoenix rising from ashes, the wheel, the bell, and the compass were retrieved from the wreck. The wheel is displayed in the Two Harbour Lighthouse Museum. The bell is aboard *Grampa Woo III*.

There was one negative effect. The licence for *Grampa Woo III* to take cruises and fishing and diving charters to Isle Royale National Park was rescinded. *Grampa Woo II*, with its rear-end on the rocks and nose in the water, surrounded by its flotsam beached on the shore, was regarded as debris, as litter. Litter is not tolerated on Isle Royale.

"No different than if somebody drove a boat up onto the rocks and left it. *Grampa Woo* is broken into five pieces plus loose plates. It is sitting in 35 feet of water and the chances are it will stay there. It is no different than litter and has no potential as a shipwreck. It has little integrity left."[38]

What happens to *Grampa Woo II* is out of Dana's hands and is now the responsibility of his insurance company. Whether or not *Grampa Woo III* will ever be welcome to Isle Royale will be reviewed.

Ironically, Gerry Dawson won the salvage contract. With his love of Lake Superior and his concern for the environment, will he consider sinking it in Canadian waters? Isle Royale Superintendent Douglas Barnard is watching.

"No, It cannot be sunk in U.S. waters. I wouldn't want to see it sunk in Canadian waters either, especially in a

National Marine Conservation Area. I would hope it would be broken up, brought in, and sold for scrap."[39]

There was little fanfare for the *Westfort* when it returned to base. Their first job was to unload equipment they had stored on the *Glenada* to facilitate stability on its return voyage.

"There was a gang of people, family, so we just came in alongside and pulled out all our stuff. We didn't actually have a chance to say goodbye; there was a lot of commotion going on. We came back to our base and there was nobody around. So, there was just the three of us. So, we said, 'Oh well, we made it back, you know.' That's what it's all about, doing the job and getting back."[40]

No doubt, in the back of their mind was the old saying of American Coast Guard crews:

"They say we have to go out, but no-one says anything about coming back."[41]

The lack of immediate attention did not particularly bother the *Westfort* crew, but there were some sardonic chuckles about the timing of their seasonal layoff notices.

"Talk about unsung heroes. After all this adrenaline pumping and being there in perilous conditions, you come home and there's no party. Well, ya, we got our layoff slips. We were gone three days, and actually, when we came back that night, our layoff notices were sitting on our desks saying that our services were no longer required as of whatever the date. They were closing down the season. So, when we came back our welcoming committee was ourselves. We shook each other's hands. That's something we get used to, because most of the stuff that we do we don't tell anybody about, the Search and Rescue people. We'll do all kinds of rescues and it won't get into newspapers at all. We don't promote ourselves."[42]

Since the "situation" of October 30, there have been changes. The hatch for the buoyancy chamber which filled with water was repaired. Prepared meals in foil pouches are now standard equipment, no longer the previous lifeboat rations. A replacement ship is apparently imminent. Originally designed and built by Textron Marine & Land Systems quartered in Louisiana, the new ship will be longer, wider, heavier, and more powerful than the *Westfort*. It will be built in Kingston, Ontario, with Canadian adaptations.

"The 47 foot Motor Lifeboat combines speed and agility to perform as a heavy weather patrol and rescue craft. Now in production for the (U.S.) Coast Guard, it also features superior survivability. Speed is 25 knots and range is 220 nautical miles."[43]

"Much more sturdy."[44]

With thoughts to the future, Coast Guard Case Number 2420 was closed.

"We were back to normalcy within a couple of hours. Rescued a guy off the breakwall the next day."[45]

Inga finished out the following season by working on the CCGC *Waubuno* on Lake Winnipeg and then taking winter employment as leader of an implementation team for a Critical Incident Stress Program. Five Coast Guard radio sites from central Lake Huron to Lake Winnipeg were consolidated into the Marine Communications and Traffic Services in Thunder Bay. Jim Harding got his captain's papers. Gerry's business has stayed steady.

"People on the lakers and that [they] never even heard of it in the Toronto area and down there."[46]

In 1997, his company moved 447 ships, an increase of 87 over the previous year. Sharon Dawson acknowledges there is "significant change from year to year."[47]

Onboard the *Glenada*, there was some remodelling. The fuel filtration system was improved, and the forward deck replaced with a grating to help prevent icing.

Because of the life-threatening experience, there were adjustments to be made in the psyches of all the individuals involved. There were adjustments to be made because of the publicity—and there were continuing deep adjustments needed as the ground swell of recognition at the western end of Lake Superior spread through the land.

Nevertheless, the crew joked about it.

"I mean, why are all these people interested in what the heck we do for a living?"[48]

9 ~ WHAT IS A HERO?

Man is amazing, but he is not a masterpiece.

Oddly enough, a hero can be classified with a scapegoat or a criminal. All are teaching tools for society.

"Be like this."

"Don't be like that."

Heroes are proclaimed as ideals, as models. They are centred out as examples, as magnets to draw people towards the kind of behaviour society wants. Designations of hero, scapegoat and criminal are the embodiment of what society wants people to be or not to be. Metonymy is a figure of speech defined by James Thurber as the "Container of the Thing Contained."[1] "It is Dr. So-and-So's office calling." Obviously the office is not making the phone call, yet the word is used because it encloses the doctor, the receptionist and everything involved. Consider the Governor General's medals. Obviously the medals are not his, or hers. It is the office and the medals which supposedly contain what society wants.

More than just metonymy, the ceremonial presentation of awards are today's morality plays. They are like the courts. What society holds dear is rewarded; what it despises is punished.[2] What is unimportant is ignored. A value judgement is reflected in medals presented for saving human life. A judgement is reflected in medals and honourary degrees presented for furthering exploration and research. A judgement is reflected in any honouring of excellence. Similarily, the value of women and children are reflected in the length of sentences meted out to their abusers.

The scapegoat, a lesser outcast than a criminal, provides a force field of public opinion, usually in the form of jokes around what society regards as negative behaviour. Sometimes these jokes reflect a covert enviousness of power or wealth, as exemplified in the jokes about doctors and lawyers—pre-millenium scapegoats. For instance, lawyers are reviled—yet envied—for their tenacity, ferocity and success:

"What is the difference between a lawyer and a pit bull?
A lawyer has two legs."

All labels are difficult for the individuals involved. Anyone with an unblinkered sense of reality or a semblance of a sense of humour cannot truly believe society's labels. No-one deserves the designation one hundred percent. Nobody is perfect. Rarely is anyone all bad.

Roberta Bondar and Terry Fox are two acknowledged heroes in a rather sparse field of identified Canadian heroes. Although not yet widely recognized—but definitely officially acknowledged—Gerry Dawson and his crew share many similarities and may well eventually stand with them.

Both Bondar and Fox gradually had hero status imposed on them as they worked and strived, one studying and experimenting, the other training and training, then running, running, running. Roberta Bondar fulfilled an early dream of space travel by undertaking a tortuous trail of university and medical degrees and speciality certificates.[3] Her articulateness, her sensitivity towards the planet Earth, her representation of capable women—and men— everywhere, still continues to expand her hero status.

Two years after Terry Fox, at the age of 19, had his leg amputated because of cancer, he started training to run across Canada. He logged over 3,000 miles. His goal of running from the Atlantic to the Pacific was halted outside Thunder Bay because of a recurrence of cancer.[4] However, his striving, his indomitability, his altruism, all focussed on raising money to help others, were the real achievements. Because people recognized this, he became a hero. The money for cancer research just keeps on coming and coming.

Involved in the achievement of the goal of Bondar, Fox and Dawson were preparation, risk, altruism, cooperation, judgement, and Sharon Dawson's *SISU*, guts, in varying combinations. The criterion for hero status seems to involve an attempt to overcome a shared fear, a societal bugaboo, an ogre in the closet, something 'out there,' nature, a pathogen, death. In fact, hero status really begins with the surmounting of human frailty and limitations.

Both Terry Fox and Roberta Bondar overcame human limitation. They worked; they risked themselves and their reputation; they cooperated with others; they used judgement; they cared about others; and they showed guts in the trying.

So Gerry Dawson. So his crew. They did what they had never done before, nosed up to a maniacal ship in huge waves and pulled two men off. Gerry risked his ship, his own life, the life of each crewman and his reputation. He used judgement in what he attempted to do. The crew cooperated with each other. They cared about saving others. They were prepared for the test. They had the guts to try.

"If we had to go again, we'd go."[5]

All three were what you might call 'sheet lightning heroes.' Their decision time was just slightly longer than for individuals who are forced to decide with the speed of fork lightning, say, to pull someone from a burning truck. A year and-a-half after the *Glenada* rescued the men from the drifting ship, Jim Hamilton and Jim Loppacher saved someone from a burning truck in an almost reflexive, instantaneous action. All these individuals unknowingly were facing an assessment of their self-worth and a crucial point in the direction of their lives. They were tested. They met the challenge. The decisions they made were a result of who they were. The difference was the speed of the decision, the speed of the reasoning process. Bondar and Fox had a fairly long consideration time; but the process was the same.

Brave and altruistic actions are not rare. A fight is stopped on a subway train. A drowning person is saved. A boater in distress is helped. Those who intervened are brave, but not heroes. Why? Not because the action was inadequate. But simply because the action was not recognized. Hero status involves recognition.

In the cases of Roberta Bondar and Terry Fox, their actions have been acknowledged on a national and international scale. Although Gerry Dawson and his crew fought and surmounted their human limitations *that night*, widespread recognition is only the beginning. Whether their competence and bravery become extensive role models for action, even beyond the medal presentations, is yet to be determined.

There is another difference between Gerry and his crew and Robert Bondar and Terry Fox. The *Glenada* crew had a sudden call on their talents as part of their routine job. They did not realize what they had done would be regarded as extraordinary. The ensuing status of hero was thrust unexpectedly upon them. Beginning with phone calls from the media even before they returned from Tee Harbour, the interest in the story just kept spreading. Bondar and Fox were able to get used to the idea gradually. Gerry and his crew were taken aback, unprepared.

They were doing their job as they always did. The "situation" became more dicey than usual, yes, but they remained cool and worked it through. When Gerry realized Jim was at risk, that there was no hope in getting a line to the stranded ship, that the life rafts were a death threat to the *Grampa Woo* captives, that there was no other ship and possibly not even a helicopter to rescue the men, he was faced with a momentous decision. *Agony of collision.* He called on his experience, on his lifelong knowledge from his family background, his mother, brother and father, his feeling of security in the preparedness of his ship and his crew, his self-worth reinforced by a strong home life; and he made, with Jim's concurrence, a plan. Jim again went out on the tilting, ice-covered, sloshing deck. In a unique moment of cooperation between nature and human, when the *Glenada* closed in on *Grampa Woo*—the gears a-going backwards, forwards, backwards, forwards, every two seconds—Lake Superior mysteriously lulled. The scissoring of the two ships stopped, and Jim grabbed the men off.

"It was probably the one and only shot. I mean, we could have tried doing it all night long."[6]

As much as Gerry's ability to work with the Lake, to make the danger-filled decision to get up tight to a big, wobbling ship, his decision to stop, to abort the recovery of that ship demonstrated his judgement as a mariner.

"I know when not to push the Lake."[7]

Human lives had become the concern. With the seas increasing, Jim, on the front line of the ice-covered bow, was pushing his luck. Jack, overcome with fumes and in his bunk, was unable to monitor the engine, the filters possibly allowing a return of water or sludge into the gas. The *Westfort*, determined to stand by, may have eventually rolled over because of its loss of buoyancy and icing. All three ships were being swept farther and farther away from a safe port. Eight lives and three ships easily could have been lost!

When recognition came, the concept of hero status was a surprise.

It was difficult being treated differently, centred out, the hard glare of publicity searching for flaws, the RCMP investigating before the big medals were presented, the flashbacks and what-ifs and recriminations and fears about what might have been. Because Gerry and his crew had a sound grasp of reality, even the thought of hero-status was difficult to accept.

"I don't think of myself as a hero or what I've done as being any different than anyone else would do. Besides, having people like Jack and Jim around I don't have a chance to have much of an ego."[8]

Gerry's wife Sharon noticed that "...in the beginning, he found it difficult, the guilt."[9] The fully-lit cruise ship

Captain Gerry Dawson with his proud mother, Wealthy Dawson, at one of the many awards presentations.

wobbling away in the night. The risk to Jim. The risk to all. The impact of the success of the hair-breadth rescue had not hit him. He was reeling from the narrow escape of possibly losing lives and ships.

"But no, he certainly doesn't put himself on a pedestal at all. He still kind of keeps shaking his head, thinking that he just did something that he would hope somebody would do for him if he was out there distressed. He went out there because he wanted to help. He thought it would be a routine rescue and he would be back in a few hours. No. I haven't seen any major changes. If there are, they would be for the good. He's kind of almost mellowed. Yes, more self-confident."[10]

Sharon conceded he had some difficulty in handling stress after *that night*.

For Jim, at 34 the youngest of the crew and father of Iain, only two years old, the experience clung to him like a bad dream. He felt resentment at being "heroed" for what was a private moment of agony. He saw himself as "a victim of circumstance," having to face the impossible choice of risking his responsibilities as a father against the plight of two stranded men, neither choice being clear-cut. The thought of turning away from the stranded men was "extraordinary," even not being able to help earlier made him feel "crappy." Yet, Iain was constantly on his mind as he fought against going overboard.

"I feel quite guilty about the whole thing. Why? Cause it was really dangerous and I don't know whether or not I had the right to do that. But then again, I don't know how I would have felt if I hadn't have done as much as I could and something would have happened to those people on that boat."[11]

In the months after the rescue, Jim lost his ability to focus. He was unable to deal with stress. But, he focussed enough to make a major decision. He sought counselling. Once diagnosed as having post-traumatic stress disorder, not a brain tumour as he had thought, his recovery began immediately.

For Jack, at 61, the old-timer of the "boys" as he calls them, his greatest pride was for his kids.

"The nicest thing about this is that it's something for my kids. I have a tendency just to forget it. It's just something that happened. It's not as if I was on a mountain. There I'd be the rescued, not the rescuer."[12]

Captain Smyth of the *McCarthy* firmly denies any hero status, despite what has been called "masterful shiphandling"[13] in bridling the bucking *Grampa Woo* and towing it to a relay point for final rescue.

"I wasn't risking my life, the ship I was on is 1000 feet long. Sure it was a delicate operation, but it wasn't like I had a choice. The real heroes are the crews of the other boats. They did risk their lives. I only risked my career. Any other Great Lakes captain would have done the same thing."[14]

Most of all, though, Gerry, his crew, and no doubt Captain Smyth, all know they must never believe the hero hype. They must stay real. Any human being who deigns to tangle with Lake Superior has to be humble to survive. Gerry and his crew cannot pay attention to adulation. They cannot have pride. They cannot believe what is being said. Quite apart from the intrinsic comedy of the human being, these men understand the puniness of the individual on or beside Lake Superior; the glitter of any medal, however grand, is neither impressive nor important. Pride has no place on the Lake.

Westfort crew, Inga Thorsteinson, Chief Coxswain Bob King, and crew Willie Trognitz receive individual awards for seamanship and bravery from ISMA Lodge #16.

"As far as I am concerned, no-one masters Lake Superior."[15]

Like Roberta Bondar and Terry Fox, Gerry had worked at doing what he wanted to do. He worked at learning how to deal with the Lake. He has worked at living a good life, and at being a positive force in the world. To Gerry's mind, he felt he was just doing his job, so did Jim Harding and Jack Olson, so did Bob King, Willie Trognitz and Inga Thorsteinson. All were experienced, all had striven to learn and understand; none were afraid of labour. Gerry had the security of a good marriage at which he also had worked, and when suddenly the job situation became extreme, they all knew what to do. Jack had his preparation beforehand, cleaning the sludge from the dirty fuel, readying the ship to withstand the extreme forces it met; Jim knew his role, no matter how dangerous or unpleasant. Gerry understood all their strengths and weaknesses, his own, the ship's, and the crew's.

The International Ship Masters Association Grand Lodge Award for Bravery and the Harbour Man of the Year Award (ISMA Lodge #16) presented by Past Grand President, Captain George Ferguson (right) to Captain Gerry Dawson.

With humility, Captain Gerry Dawson accepts the John T. Saunders Award for Outstanding Performance, Twin Ports Lodge #12. Duluth/ Superior, presented by Captain Robert Libby.

"When everything's going right, the job looks boring."[16]

But they could never know what to expect.

Jim was knocked unconscious from a line from a saltie, was almost "squished" between two ships, (not when Gerry was at the helm). Gerry lost the tip of one finger and damaged two others.

"Jim almost had things thrown on him; just get a little wind, weather and ice mixed in there and something can happen in a split second."[17]

Then along comes the *Grampa Woo*.
They were ready.

"The hero is a man of self-achieved submission. But submission to what? That precisely is the riddle that today we have to ask ourselves and that it is everywhere the primary virtue and historic deed of the hero to have solved."[18]

Gerry Dawson, Jim Harding, and Jack Olson on the *Glenada*, Bob King, Willie Trognitz, and Inga Thorsteinson on the *Westfort* waiting to help, solved the riddle on October 30, 1996. They stand for all the other mariners both today and in the past who have submitted with humility and respect to the grandeur and power of the sea.

They may be the most important heroes society has.

Crew Jim Harding and Engineer Jack Olson received individual awards for bravery and a plaque honouring the *Glenada*. These were presented by First Vice-President, Peter Porichuk and Captain George Ferguson, ISMA Lodge #16.

OFFICIAL RECOGNITION[19]

Awards to Captain Gerry Dawson, M.B.

~ Governor General's Medal of Bravery. Notification, September 10, 1998. Presentation June, 1999.

~ International Ship Masters Association (ISMA) Grand Lodge Award for Bravery presented by Past Grand President, Captain George Ferguson and Lodge #16 First Vice President, Peter Porichuk, "for their courage and seamanship," February 28, 1997.

~ Citizens of Exceptional Achievement for Outstanding Acts of Heroism, City of Thunder Bay, "Captain Dawson performed a masterful act of seamanship in saving the lives of these men and deserves recognition along with his two crew members," February 26, 1998.

~ Harbour Man of the Year, ISMA, Lodge #16, presented by Past Grand President, Captain George Ferguson, assisted by First Vice President, Peter Porichuk, Thunder Bay, Ontario, "for his courage and seamanship," February 28, 1997.

~ John T. Saunders Award for Outstanding Performance, ISMA, Twin Ports Lodge #12, Duluth/Superior, presented by Captain Robert Libby, Thunder Bay, "to recognize outstanding professionalism in the marine field," February 28, 1997.

~ ISMA Twin Ports Lodge #12 Award for Bravery, Thunder Bay, Ontario, February 28, 1997.

~ United States Coast Guard Public Service Commendation, Cleveland 9th District, endorsed by Rear Admiral, G.F. Woolever, and presented by Commander Alan Moore, for "selfless display of courage and sound professional judgement ... in keeping with the highest traditions of the professional mariner and of the United States Coast Guard," February 28, 1997.

To Crewman Jim Harding, M.B.

~ Governor General's Medal of Bravery. Notification September 10, 1998. Presentation June, 1999.

~ ISMA Grand Lodge Award for Bravery presented by Past Grand President, Captain George Ferguson and Lodge #16 First Vice President, Peter Porichuk, February 28, 1997.

~ *ISMA Twin Ports Lodge #12 Award for Bravery, on February 28, 1997.

~ United States Coast Guard Public Service Commendation, Cleveland 9th District, endorsed by Rear Admiral, G.F. Woolever, and presented by Commander Alan Moore, February 28, 1997.

To Chief Engineer Jack Olson, M.B.

~ Governor General's Medal of Bravery. Notification September 10, 1998. Presentation June, 1999.

To Captain Gerry Dawson of the *Glenada*, and crew, Chief Engineer Jack Olson, and crewman Jim Harding:

~ Thunder Bay Harbour Commission Award for Exemplary Seamanship and Bravery, presented by Dennis Johnson, Harbour Commissioner, Keefer Terminal, Thunder Bay, November, 1996.

~ Canadian Coast Guard Commissioner's Commendation, Sarnia, Ontario, for "bravery, dedication, and profession-alism," March, 1997.

To Chief Coxswain Bob King of the *Westfort*, and crewmen Inga Thorsteinson and Willie Trognitz:

~ ISMA Lodge #16, individual awards for Seamanship and Bravery from, February 28, 1997;

~ Canadian Coast Guard Commendation, Sarnia, February, 1997.

To Captain Lawrence (Larry) Smyth:

~ United States Coast Guard Special Service Commendation 9th District, presented by Rear Admiral Gerald Woolever, Cleveland, Ohio, January 29, 1997. "The USCG firmly believes Smyth's actions saved the lives of two men in what has been described as 'one of the most harrowing at-sea rescues in recent Great Lakes history.'"[20]

TRIBUTES

Engineer Rolland Frayne
They did a marvellous job and I'm very proud of them for doing what they did.

Gene Onchulenko
There is a feeling amongst the senior people in the marine fraternity, that, "This is seamanship, this is bravery."

Captain Fred Broennle
An extremely brave act of seamanship. To put the bow up against another ship in a raging sea...You always have to go that little way beyond when there's people. Those people would have just vanished.

Harbour Master Dennis Johnson
It was a storm that gave me the willies. Three or four metre waves. A dark night, absolutely no visibility.

Alexander Paterson
A super achievement. Superhuman. I'm glad he's not a braggart sort of guy because it adds to the mystique.

Captain Jack Gurney
A wild, wild night. What he did, few other people would do. An amazing job.

Captain Roger Hurst
It can get rough out there and he did a good job.

Germaine Kangas
I felt the story really needed to be told.

AFTERWORD

This wonder; this masterpiece of Nature.

Rescue from Grampa Woo is a story about heroism. It is a story about many heroes, one in particular, who worked with Lake Superior to save two lives. He and his crew have received one of the highest honours in the land, the Governor General's Medal of Bravery.

Rescue from Grampa Woo is a mariner's story, a sea story, a tale of adventure, risk, and dedication.

As well, *Rescue from Grampa Woo* is a story about what could be called *the experience of North*, the longing for—and realization of—something inexpressible, something intangible that seems to be found in the swirling mystique of Lake Superior. For many, it can be found in the woods, in the water of a transparent lake, in the space and vistas of the totality of existence of which the human is only a part.

Here, clock-time can disappear. Singular constructs like time and space become inter-dimensional. There is a swaying forwards and backwards into what seems to be other realities. There can be a kinship with everything, with tussocks of blonde grasses, with a stock-still moose its ears periscoping forward, with a splash from a wave pirouetting in the sun.

North is usually regarded as that other part of Canada beyond the two hundred mile swath of cities, farms, and industry along the border. The near North is somewhere beyond the big cities. The far North, everyone knows, extends to the white of the North Pole. Few know it is possible to stand in twenty-four time zones at once and watch the sun make an orbit parallel to the horizon.[1]

About the North, wherever it is, there is mystery and fear. Just as 'out West' once connoted pioneering, enterprise, and excitement, 'up North' connotes a life-style, an attitude, a direction in living, which is more than a point on the compass. The experience of this, *the experience of North*, is a feeling.

It may be unconscious psychological accuracy that causes Americans to dub the wild, steep beauty of the western shore of Lake Superior 'the North shore.'

John Flood, editor and publisher, of Penumbra Press calls it "northness." He founded his publishing house, Penumbra Press, and the periodical, *Northward Journal*, to articulate this "northness." Although award-winning and of the highest quality, *Northward Journal* is now defunct, and Penumbra Press is just surviving, probably because the experience of this northness has only begun to be recognized in literature. It has long been articulated visually, and recognized lustily, in the art of Tom Thomson, the Group of Seven and its followers. Not so in literature.

John Flood's endeavours may be struggling because there is a somewhat pejorative, hiddenly disdainful, attitude towards the North. To most urbanites, *their* education, *their* culture, *their* life style, is simply the best. The easy casualness outside big cities, other than in seasonal cottage country, is simply below them.

Yet, the stories, the adventures, the personalities, are there. Logging, mining, homesteading, the creation of a culture that protects and nourishes the inhabitants, are an important part, like it or not, of the Canadian psyche. The lifestyle and personalities in *Rescue from Grampa Woo* reflect a piece of this importance.

Without articulation in literature, the events and experiences of northness will never enter into our collective imagination. It may never be understood how Northern lands—near and far—shaped its people, how its people shaped the land. Something could be irreparably lost. Gerry Dawson would just become another name on a list.

Fortunately, Barry Penhale of Natural Heritage is beginning to plumb the depths of *the experience of North* and could be on the way to establishing a literary genre similar to those for the prairies and the east coast and southern Ontario. He accepted the manuscript for *Rescue from Grampa Woo* with much interest, a happy event for the author as Natural Heritage was her first choice.

In some of the American states which border the Great Lakes, a recognition of a genre seems to be developing. Editor Victoria Brehm received a sizeable National Endowment for the Humanities grant to compile two anthologies of Great Lakes native writing. *The Women's Great Lakes Reader* was recently published by Holy Cow! Press in Duluth, Minnesota, and the University of Minnesota is compiling an *Encyclopedia of the Seas and the Great Lakes*. The author is included in the latter two.

Glenn Gould tried to catch *the experience of North* in his somewhat perplexing three-part CBC radio series, *The Idea of North*. So much did he value this nebulousness, he attempted to create almost a new art form to express it.[2]

Kids understand. They understand, not in words, but in their actions. Put them on the shore of Lake Superior and watch them. They skitter over the lichen-covered rocks; they climb the unique shapes of wind-bonsaied trees; they collect pretty stones not realizing they are agate and jasper and tigers eye; they hopscotch and balance and shriek. Eventually, if it is warm, they shed their clothes, first their shoes and socks, to wade over unslippery, algae-free rocks, watching their toes dance in the crystalline water, then off come their jeans and shirts for total immersion. A proto-type of baptism in what is truly the water of life. The thought is shattered when the children involuntarily yelp what is called "the Lake Superior scream."

Not just northerners know. Those who do rarely talk about it. They participate in it, sometimes constructively in a protective, stewardship kind of way, often times just passively enjoying, listening, feeling, being. Or sometimes they participate in the under-belly of northness, with rampant, often economically motivated, destruction, desecration and depletion. Polluting. Bear-baiting. Clear-cutting.

For everyone who lives in the North, near and far, survival is a constant consideration. Eyelashes freeze to faces in the cold; exhaust fumes obscure visibility; a walk in the woods could be a path to James Bay. Snow often requires shovelling or ploughing twice a day. There are road wash-outs, bears, moose, mice, mosquitoes. With all this goes an invisible badge of toughness—of guts—they all know they wear.

"Suffering confers identity. It makes you proud."[3]

They boast that mudslides and tornadoes and floods, earthquakes, wars, and traffic and crime are little known in the North. Such may or may not be true.

Both northerners and urbanites covertly eye each other somewhat disparagingly. Each feels a sense of superiority over their counterpart. But neither is whole without the other. Urbanites can lack soul if they never know the *experience of North*. Northerners, if lacking exposure to art, music, museums, and architecture, never know the expansive and thrilling insights wrought by the critical mass of people called civilization.

Of course, a person does not have to live in the North to feel the *experience of North*. In the wind tunnels of downtown Toronto, a shaft of sun-light penetrating the grey can provide transportation to this nether existence.

The experience of North is a nebulousness that defies categorization, a freedom, a dance of life, a respect, rare and special and almost requiring, as Glenn Gould thought, a special art form to express it. Almost. Written, artistic, photographic, and musical articulation will do.

Rescue from Grampa Woo is a story about people who touch and know and live in the near north. Inga of the Coast Guard, who as a youngster in Winnipeg used to race a 400 passenger riverboat in her rowboat, and now revels in rowing her hand-made wherry in the chop of Lake Superior. Seventy-two year old Wealthy, who calmly took photos of a forest fire as it approached her and her grandson because she was confident in her escape plan, and who as a young married woman heaved up lines from a floating convenience store, called a Bum Boat, to freighters in order to sell tuck to ship-bound sailors. Sharon who luxuriates in the scene of ships and water as she drives towards Lake Superior on Red River Road in Thunder Bay. Gerry, her husband, a tugboat captain, who wants to be nowhere else but on the Lake, the same Gerry, who risked his life for others as he fought his human limitations in dealing with the power of one of the symbols of *experience of North*: Lake Superior. Dana, the captain of a million dollar cruise ship, who steps on his ship in the early morning and raises his arms to the sun and says: "I love my job!"

Such articulation reveals an exciting slice of *this experience of the North*. Perhaps more.

EPILOGUE

This story has a happy ending in many ways. There was no loss of life. All involved met the challenge of hazardous circumstances. The stately *Grampa Woo III* now sails the western coast of Lake Superior. The wreck of *Grampa Woo II* was not sunk in the Lake. Its 45 tons of debris was towed to Thunder Bay and sold as scrap. The crew of the *Glenada* received letters from Rideau Hall, Ottawa, informing them they were recipients of the Governor General's Medal of Bravery, one of three decorations for bravery instituted in 1972 by Her Majesty the Queen on the advice of the Canadian Government. These medals are among "The highest accolades Canada can bestow."[1] Captain Gerry Dawson, chief engineer Jack Olson, crewman Jim Hardy are now entitled to use the letters M.B. after their name.

The first of three barge-loads of scrap that was once *Grampa Woo II* was towed to Keefer Terminal in June, 1998, by one of Captain Gerry Dawson's companies, Thunder Bay Marine Services.

The *Glenada* and *Westfort* sought shelter in the lee of Turtlehead, the misty headland at the northern tip of Pie Island. Here they "hid" from the storm until they could take over the towing of *Grampa Woo* from the *Walter J. McCarthy Jr.*

Magical light.

Lake Superior inspires respect and fun. Dr. Lee Kurisko and his niece, Carla Hunt, know.

The cobalt blue of Lake Superior.

Children shed their clothes to romp in Lake Superior. Jeffrey Wiebe-Connolly and Samantha Connolly and Kaïja.

The rocks turn molten orange.

Rock, sky, water and wind.

A confused sea.

NOTES

Chapter One: The Beginning

[1] Inga Thorsteinson, March 6, 1997.
[2] Captain Gerry Dawson, Thunder Bay Kiwanis Club, April 24, 1997.
[3] —— *Soundings*. American Steamship Company, January 1997, Volume 16, Number 3, p.1
[4] Stanley Dawson, April 15, 1997.
[5] Bob King, April 1, 1997.
[6] Inga Thorsteinson, March 6, 1997.
[7] Jack Olson, February 24, 1997.
[8] Jim Harding, April 14, 1997
[9] Ibid.
[10] Gerry Dawson, March 6, 1997.
[11] Jim Harding, April 14, 1997.
[12] Bob King, April 1, 1997.
[13] Inga Thorsteinson, March 6, 1997.
[14] Ibid.
[15] Bob King, April 1, 1997.
[16] Inga Thorsteinson, March 6, 1997.
[17] Robin Sivill, May 31, 1997.
[18] Ibid, September 15, 1997.

Chapter Two: The Eighth Sea

[1] —— *The Great Lakes, An Environmental Atlas and Resource Book*. Environment Canada, United States Environmental Protection Agency, Brock University, Northwestern University, 1988, p. 4.
[2] Verna Mize, as quoted by Barbara Stanton, in the *Detroit Free Press*, Special Issue, August 8, 1981, p. 34
[3] Elaine Morgan, *The Descent of Woman, The Aquatic Ape*. (Stein and Day Publishers, 1972).
[4] Gerry Dawson, June 19, 1997.
[5] Captain Dana Kollars, May 31, 1997.
[6] Rolland Frayne, January 27, 1998.
[7] —— *A Field Guide to Aquatic Exotic Plants and Animals*, Lake Superior Management Unit. (Not dated.)
[8] *Guide to Eating Ontario Sport Fish*. (18th edition revised) Ministry of Energy and Environment, Queen's Printer. (Not dated.)
[9] Captain Dana Kollars, September 7, 1997.
[10] Captain Gerry Dawson, June 11, 1997.

[11] —— *Northern Wood Preservers Site Remediation Plan*. Acres International Ltd., in association with Chester Environmental Ltd. Ministry of the Environment, Thunder Bay, Ontario, 1993; p. 2-2.

[12] Herbert W. Bergson, Mayor, Superior, Wisconsin, January 18, 1995. Bob Hartley, Chair, Public Advisory Committee, Thunder Bay Remedial Action Plan, May 1, 1995.

[13] Captain Gerry Dawson, June 19, 1997.

[14] Jim Bailey, Lake Superior Programs, March 13, 1998.

[15] Jake Vander Wal, manager, Lake Superior Programs, June 3, 1998.

[16] —— *Eagle Project, 7–Year Summary Report*, 1990–1997, p.24.

[17] —— *Focus*, International Joint Commission, Special Issue on Great Lakes Areas of Concern, March/April, 1998, p.6.

[18] Captain Gerry Dawson, February 15, 1997.

[19] Captain Dana Kollars, May 31, 1997.

[20] Ibid, September 7, 1997.

[21] Gerry Dawson, February 15, 1997.

[22] Captain Stan Dawson, April 15, 1997.

[23] J.E. Lovelock, *Gaia: A New Look At Life On Earth*. (Oxford, Oxford University Press), 1991.

[24] Captain Gerry Dawson, February 15, 1997.

[25] The Rev. George Grant, diarist of Sanford Fleming's 1872 Canadian expedition, as quoted in the *Detroit Free Press*, Special Issue, August 9, 1981, p. 1.

[26] —— *The Great Lakes, An Environmental Atlas and Resource Book*. Environment Canada, United States Environmental Protection Agency, Brock University, Northwestern University, 1988, p. 7.

[27] Ibid.

[28] E.G. Pye, *Geology and Scenery, North Shore of Lake Superior*. Ontario Department of Mines, Geological Guide Book No. 2, 1969, p. 27.

[29] Howard Bell. "Superior Pursuit, Facts About the Greatest Great Lake," *Superior Advisory Notes*, Minnesota Sea Grant Extenion, University of Minnesota, 1985.

[30] Bruce Littlejohn and Wayland Drew, *Superior: The Haunted Shore*. (Toronto, Gage, 1975), p. 27.

[31] —— *The Archeology of North Central Ontario, Prehistoric Cultures North of Superior*. Ministry of Culture and Recreation, 1981, p. 4.

[32] R.S. MacNeish, "A Possible Early Site in the Thunder Bay District, Ontario." National Museum of Canada Bulletin, No. 126, Ottawa, 1952, pp 23-49.

[33] —— *The Great Lakes, An Environmental Atlas and Resource Book*. Environment Canada, United States Environmental Protection Agency, Brock University, Northwestern University, 1988, p. 16; —Dictionary of Canadian Biography, Vol. 1., (University of Toronto Press, 1966), p. 554.

[34] Howard Bell, "Superior Pursuit, Facts about the Greatest Great Lake," *Superior Advisory Notes*. Minnesota Sea Grant Extenion, University of Minnesota, 1985.

[35] —— *Currents*, Lake Superior Center, Winter, 1997.

[36] Ibid.

[37] Nancy Nelson. "Clearly Superior" *Seiche*. Minnesota Sea Grant, University of Minnesota (March, 1998), p. 6.

[38] —— *The Great Lakes, An Environmental Atlas and Resource Book*. Environment Canada, United States Environmental Protection Agency, Brock University, Northwestern University, 1988, p. 29.

[39] Ibid. pp.3-4.

[40] Dr. Michael J. McCormick, NOAA Great Lakes Environmental Research Lab, Ann Arbor, Michigan, March 11, 1998.

[41] E.G. Bennett, 1978, "Characteristics of the Thermal Regime of Lake Superior," *Journal of Great Lakes Research*. E.B. Bennett, 1978, "Climate Normals," *Journal of Great Lakes Research*.

[42] Ibid.

[43] Dr. Joseph MacInnis, *Fitzgerald's Storm, The Wreck of the Edmund Fitzgerald*. (Toronto, MacMillan Canada, 1979), p. 42.

[44] Captain Gerry Dawson, June 19, 1997.

[45] —— *The Great Lakes, An Environmental Atlas and Resource Book*, 1988, p. 4.

[46] Howard Bell, "Superior Pursuit, Facts about the Greatest Great Lake," *Superior Advisory Notes*. Minnesota Sea Grant Extension, University of Minnesota, 1985.

[47] Ibid.

[48] Ibid.

[49] Ibid.

[50] T. Virene, August 29, 1997.

[51] Dr. Werner Beyer, October, 1997.

[52] T. Virene, August 29, 1997.

[53] *Sault Star*, July 15, 1995.

[54] *The Great Lakes Reporter*, September/October, 1992.

[55] Captain Gerry Dawson, March 3, 1998.

[56] Ibid, March 11, 1997.

[57] Ibid, speech at Thunder Bay Kiwanis Club, April 24, 1997.

[58] Ibid.

[59] Ibid.

[60] Joan Skelton, *The Survivor of the Edmund Fitzgerald*. (Moonbeam, Ont., Penumbra Press, 1985).

[61] Julius F. Wolff Jr., *Lake Superior Shipwrecks*. (Duluth, Minnesota, Lake Superior Port Cities, 1990), pp. 119, 124.

[62] Ibid, p. ix.

[63] Captain Stanley Dawson, April 15, 1997.

[64] William Bridgewater and Semour Kurtz, (Editors), *Columbia Encyclopedia*, 1956.

[65] W.T.R. Allen, *Wind and Sea*: State of sea photographs for the Beaufort wind scale = *Le vent et la mer*: photographies de l'état de la mer pour l'échelle de Beaufort, (Downsview). Environment Canada, Atmospheric Environment Service, 1983.

[66] Ibid.

[67] Ibid.

[68] —— *Soundings*, American Steamship Company, January 1997, Volume 16, Number 3, p. 1.

[69] *U.S.C.G. Marine Casualty Narrative Supplement*, "Grampa Woo Grounding," December 8, 1997.

[70] Julie Turner, Environment Canada, Thunder Bay, April 20, 1988.

[71] Sebastian Junger, *The Perfect Storm*. (New York, W.W. Thorton, 1997), p. 119.

[72] Ibid.

[73] Inga Thorsteinson, June 22, 1997.

[74] —— *Science Dimension*, 1979/3, p. 30.

[75] Frederick Stonehouse, *Went Missing*. (AuTrain, Michigan; Avery Color Studios, 1977).

[76] Sebastian Junger, *The Perfect Storm*. p. 153.

[77] Crew Willie Trognitz, June 22, 1997; Captain Fred Broennle, January 3, 1998.

[78] Captain Gerry Dawson, June 11, 1997.

[79] Captain Stan Dawson, April 15, 1997.

Chapter Three: The Women In His Life

[1] Captain Gerry Dawson, February 27, 1997.

[2] Sharon Dawson, March 11, 1998.

[3] Captain Gerry Dawson, February 28, 1997.

[4] Wealthy Dawson, April 15, 1997.

[5] *Rescue from Grampa Woo*, "Afterward", p. 151

[6] Wealthy Dawson, June 27, 1997.

[7] Ibid.

[8] Ibid, April, 15, 1997.

[9] Gene Onchulenko, August 28, 1998.

[10] *Distant Voices*, TV Ontario and Sleeping Giant Productions; Paul McConvey, Producer, ca. 1990.

[11] *Distant Voices*, TV Ontario and Sleeping Giant Productions.

[12] Ibid.

[13] Ibid.

[14] Ibid.

[15] Wealthy Dawson, June 27, 1997.

[16] *Distant Voices*, TV Ontario and Sleeping Giant Productions.

[17] Wealthy Dawson, June 27, 1997.

[18] *Distant Voices*, TV Ontario and Sleeping Giant Productions.

[19] Ibid.

[20] Wealthy Dawson, June 27, 1997.

[21] Captain Gerry Dawson, February 15, 1997.

[22] Wealthy Dawson, June 27, 1997.

[23] Ibid.

[24] Ibid.

[25] Ibid.

[26] Captain Gerry Dawson, February 10, 1997.

[27] Wealthy Dawson, June 27, 1997.

[28] Ibid.

[29] Sharon Dawson, March 17, 1997.

[30] Ibid.

[31] Captain Gerry Dawson, February 10, 1997.

[32] Ibid, February 28, 1997.

[33] Sharon Dawson, March 17, 1997.

[34] Gene Onchulenko, August 28, 1998.

[35] Sharon Dawson, March 17, 1997.

[36] Ibid.

[37] Ibid.

[38] Ibid.

[39] Ibid.

[40] Ibid, June 21, 1997.

[41] Ibid.

[42] Heather Dawson, June 21, 1997.

Chapter Four: Her Soul Encoded By Water And Boats

[1] Inga Thorsteinson, April 21, 1997.

[2] Ibid, April 24, 1997.

[3] Ibid, March 6, 1997.

[4] Ibid, April 21, 1997.

[5] Ibid.

[6] Ibid.

7 Inga Thorsteinson, July, 1997.

8 Chief Coxswain Bob King, CHFD-CKPR TV.

9 Greg Sladics, January 31, 1997.

10 Thomas E. Appleton, "A History of the Canadian Coast Guard and marine Services," *Usque Ad Mare*. Department of Transport, Ottawa, 1968, pp. 133-138.

11 Greg Sladics, January 23, 1997.

12 Lieutenant Randall G. Wagner, Marine Safety Office, Duluth, Minnesota.

13 Frederick Stonehouse, *Wreck Ashore*. (Duluth (MN), Lake Superior Port Cities, 1994), p. 63.

14 *Chronicle-Journal*, April 23, 1997.

15 Inga Thorsteinson, March 6, 1997.

16 Ibid, April 21, 1997.

17 Ibid, March 6, 1997.

18 Ibid.

19 Ibid, April 21, 1997.

20 Ibid, March 6, 1997.

21 Ibid.

22 Ibid.

23 Willie Trognitz, April 7, 1997.

24 —— *44' MLB Operator's Handbook*. U.S. Department of Transportation, United States Coast Guard (Washington, D.C., 1992).

25 Inga Thorsteinson, March 3, 1998.

26 Captain Stan Dawson, April 15, 1997.

27 Chief Coxswain Bob King, April 1, 1997.

28 Willie Trognitz, April 7, 1997.

29 Ed Greer, April 21, 1997.

30 Chief Coxswain Bob King, April 1, 1997.

31 Ibid, June 9, 1997.

32 Ibid.

33 Willie Trognitz, June 9, 1997.

34 Ibid, April 7, 1997.

35 Chief Coxswain Bob King, June 9, 1997.

36 Coxswain Ed Greer, June 22, 1997.

37 Inga Thorsteinson, March 6, 1997.

38 Ibid.

39 Ibid, April 21, 1997.

[40] Ibid, March 6, 1997.

[41] Ibid, March 6, 1997.

[42] Captain Gerry Dawson, February 10, 1997.

Chapter Five: The Crew And The Ship

[1] E. Lovelock, *Gaia, A New Look at Life on Earth*. (Oxford, Oxford University Press, 1991), p. 34.

[2] Jack Olson, January 14, 1997.

[3] Ibid, February 24, 1997.

[4] Rolland Frayne, February 24, 1997.

[5] Germaine Kangas.

[6] Captain Gerry Dawson, February 15, 1997.

[7] Howard Reid's column, *Chronicle-Journal*, April 30, 1995.

[8] Jim Harding, April 14, 1997.

[9] Jack Olson, February 24, 1997.

[10] Inga Thorsteinson, February 17, 1998.

[11] Jack Olson, February 17, 1997.

[12] Ibid, January 14, 1997.

[13] Ibid, Februray 17, 1997.

[14] Ibid, February 24, 1997.

[15] Ibid.

[16] Ibid, February 17, 1997.

[17] Ibid, February 24, 1997.

[18] Jim Harding, August 14, 1997.

[19] Elinor Barr, *Silver Islet, Striking it Rich in Lake Superior*. (Toronto, Natural Heritage,1988), p. 10.

[20] Sharon Dawson, March17, 1997.

[21] Jim Harding, April 14, 1997.

[22] Captain Gerry Dawson, March 11, 1997.

[23] Ibid, February 10, 1997.

[24] Captain Stan Dawson, 1997.

[25] Captain Gerry Dawson, February 10, 1997.

[26] Ibid, March 11, 1997.

[27] Ibid, June 19, 1997.

[28] Davis Dawson, June 21, 1997.

[29] Captain Gerry Dawson, March 11, 1997.

[30] Ibid.

[31] Ibid, February 10, 1997.

[32] Ibid, March 11, 1997.

[33] Ibid, February 15, 1997.

[34] Ibid.

[35] Ibid.

[36] Sharon Dawson, March 17, 1997.

[37] Ibid.

[38] Captain Gerry Dawson, February 15, 1997.

[39] Nathan Dawson, June 21, 1997.

[40] Captain Gerry Dawson, February 15, 1997.

[41] Ibid.

[42] Wealthy Dawson, June 27, 1997.

[43] Captain Gerry Dawson, June 11, 1997.

[44] Ibid, March 11, 1997.

[45] Jim Harding, April 14, 1997.

[46] Wilbur Smith as quoted by Ben Knight in *The Readers Showcase*, Vol. 5, Issue 5, May/June, 1997.

Chapter Six: Grampa Woo

[1] —— *Soundings*, American Steamship Company, March/April, 1997, Vol. 17, Number 1, p. 1.

[2] Captain Larry Smyth, *Soundings*, American Steamship Company, January, 1997. Vol. 16, Number 3, p. 2

[3] —— *Soundings*, American Steamship Company, March/April, 1997, Vol. 17, Number 1, p. 5.

[4] Canadian Coast Guard MCTS, *Narrative Summary re: Grampa Woo*, UTC Day, October 30, 1996.

[5] ChunAe Kollars, September 15, 1997.

[6] Captain Dana Kollars, May 31, 1997.

[7] ChunAe Kollars, September 15, 1997.

[8] Captain Dana Kollars, May 31, 1997.

[9] Ibid.

[10] Ibid, September 15, 1997.

[11] Ibid, May 31, 1997.

[12] Ibid, September 15, 1997.

[13] Ibid, May 31, 1997.

[14] Ibid.

[15] Ibid.

[16] Robin Sivill, September 15, 1997.

[17] Captain Dana Kollars, September 7, 1997.

[18] Robin Sivill, September 15, 1997.

[19] Ibid.

[20] Captain Dana Kollars, May 31, 1997.

[21] Robin Sivill, September 15, 1997.

[22] Ibid.

[23] Ibid.

[24] Ibid.

[25] Lt. Randall G. Wagner, Marine Safety Office, Duluth, December 8, 1997.

[26] —— *Narrative Summary re: Grampa Woo*, Canadian Coast MCTS, June 18, 1997.

[27] ChunAe Kollars, September 15, 1997.

[28] Captain Lawrence Smyth, as quoted by John Myers in *Duluth News-Tribune*, November 1 , 1996.

[29] Gene Onchulenko, December 19, 1997.

[30] Captain Lawrence Smyth as quoted by John Meyers in *Duluth News-Tribune*, November 1, 1996.

[31] Captain Dana Kollars, May 31, 1997.

[32] Robin Sivill, September 15, 1997.

[33] Captain Dana Kollars, May 31, 1997.

[34] Robin Sivill, September 15, 1997.

[35] Ibid.

[36] Ibid.

[37] Captain Lawrence Smyth as quoted by John Meyers in *Duluth News-Tribune*, November 12, 1996.

[38] Robin Sivill, September 15, 1997.

Chapter Seven: The Longest Hour

[1] Inga Thorsteinson, personal journal, November, 1996.

[2] Chief Coxswain Bob King, April 1, 1997.

[3] Captain Gerry Dawson,. June 11, 1997.

[4] Ibid, February 15, 1997.

[5] Gene Onchulenko, December 19, 1997.

[6] Ibid.

[7] E.G. Pye, "North Shore of Lake Superior," *Geology and Scenery*. Ontario Department of Mines, 1962, p. 52.

[8] Inga Thorsteinson, June 22, 1997.

[9] Chief Coxswain Bob King, April 1, 1997.

[10] Ibid.

[11] Captain Gerry Dawson, speech at Thunder Bay Kiwanis Club, April 24, 1997.

[12] Chief Coxswain Bob King, April 1, 1997.

[13] Captain Gerry Dawson, speech at Thunder Bay Kiwanis Club, April 24, 1997.

[14] Ibid.

[15] Ibid, March 6, 1997.

[16] Ibid, speech at Thunder Bay Kiwanis Club, April 24, 1997.

[17] Ibid.

[18] Coxswain Bob King, April 1, 1997.

[19] Willie Trognitz, April 7, 1997.

[20] Captain Gerry Dawson, speech at Thunder Bay Kiwanis Club, April 24, 1997.

[21] Inga Thorsteinson, November 14, 1997.

[22] Captain Gerry Dawson, speech at Thunder Bay Kiwanis Club, April 24, 1997.

[23] Sebastian Junger, *The Perfect Storm*. (New York, W.W. Norton, 1997), p. 125.

[24] Captain Gerry Dawson, June 11, 1997.

[25] Ibid, speech at Thunder Bay Kiwanis Club, April 24, 1997.

[26] Ibid, February 15, 1997.

[27] Ibid.

[28] Ibid, speech at Thunder Bay Kiwanis Club, April 24, 1997.

[29] Ibid.

[30] Inga Thorsteinson, March 6, 1997.

[31] Canadian Coast Guard radio log, October 30, 1996.

[32] Captain Dana Kollars, KDLH-TV, Duluth,

[33] Captain Gerry Dawson, speech at Thunder Bay Kiwanis Club, April 24, 1997.

[34] Captain Dana Kollars, May 31, 1997.

[35] Captain Gerry Dawson, speech at Thunder Bay Kiwanis Club, April 24, 1997.

[36] Inga Thorsteinson, June 9, 1997.

[37] Jim Harding, April 14, 1997.

[38] Captain Gerry Dawson, February 10, 1997.

[39] Ibid, speech at Thunder Bay Kiwanis Club, April 24, 1997.

[40] Ibid, March 6, 1997.

[41] Jim Harding, April 14, 1997.

[42] Captain Gerry Dawson, speech at Thunder Bay Kiwanis Club, April 24, 1997.

[43] Jim Harding, January 10, 1998.

[44] Ibid, April 14, 1997.

[45] Captain Gerry Dawson, speech at Thunder Bay Kiwanis Club, April 24, 1997.

[46] Canadian Coast Guard radio log, October 30, 1996.

[47] Captain Gerry Dawson, March 6, 1997.

[48] Inga Thorsteinson, November 14, 1997.

[49] Chief Coxswain Bob King, April 1, 1997.

[50] Ibid.

[51] Inga Thorsteinson, November 14, 1997.

[52] Ibid.

[53] Ibid, March 3, 1998.

Chapter Eight: Afterwards

[1] Jack Olson, February 24, 1997.

[2] Captain Gerry Dawson, speech at Thunder Bay Kiwanis Club, April 24, 1997.

[3] Ibid, March 6, 1997.

[4] Ibid.

[5] Ibid, speech at Thunder Bay Kiwanis Club, April 24, 1997.

[6] Inga Thorsteinson, March 3, 1998.

[7] Canadian Coast Guard MCTS, *Narrative Summary re: Grampa Woo*. June 18, 1997, p. 12.

[8] Inga Thorsteinson, November 14, 1997.

[9] Jack Olson, February 17, 1997.

[10] Wille Trognitz, April 7, 1997.

[11] Chief Coxswain Bob King, April 1, 1997.

[12] Willie Trognitz, April 7.

[13] Inga Thorsteinson, March 6, 1997.

[14] Canadian Coast Guard MCTS, *Narrative Summary re: Grampa Woo*. June 18, 1997.

[15] Jack Olson, February 17, 1997.

[16] Jim Harding, April 14, 1997.

[17] Ibid.

[18] Alexander Paterson, December 22, 1997.

[19] Willie Trognitz, April 7, 1997.

[20] Dana Kollars, May 31, 1997.

[21] Captain Gerry Dawson, March 6, 1997.

[22] Alexander Paterson, December 22, 1997.

[23] As told to Richard Boone, CJLB, by Captain Dana Kollars, November 1, 1997.

[24] As told to David Akin by Captain Dana Kollars and published in the *Chronicle-Journal*, November 2, 1996.

[25] As told to Richard Boone, CJLB, by Captain Dana Kollars, November 1, 1997.

[26] Jim Harding, April 14, 1997.

[27] Captain Dana Kollars, September 7, 1997.

[28] Ibid.

[29] Ibid, May 31, 1997.

[30] Ibid, September 7, 1997.

[31] U.S. Coast Guard, *Marine Casualty Narrative Supplement*, December 8, 1997.

[32] Captain Dana Kollars, May 31, 1997.

[33] Ibid, September 7, 1997.

[34] Ibid.

[35] Ibid, May 31, 1997.

[36] Ibid.

[37] Ibid.

[38] Douglas Barnard, Superintendent, Isle Royale National Park, Michigan, December 1, 1997.

[39] Ibid.

[40] Chief Coxswain Bob King, April 1, 1997.

[41] Inga Thorsteinson, March 6, 1997.

[42] Chief Coxswain Bob King, April 1, 1997.

[43] —— *Sea Classics*, June 1997, Vol. 30, Number 6, p. 28.

[44] Chief Coxswain Bob King, March 22, 1998.

[45] Ibid.

[46] Captain Gerry Dawson, January 11, 1998.

[47] Sharon Dawson, March 2, 1998.

[48] Jim Harding, April 14, 1997.

Chapter Nine: What Is A Hero

[1] James Thurber, "Here Lies Miss Groby," *The Thurber Carnival*. (New York/London, Harper and Brothers, 1995), p. 52.

[2] J. Desmond Morton, *The Function of Criminal Law in 1962*. (Toronto, CBC Productions, 1962), p. 30.

[3] Shawn J., Allaire/InfoTech Services. September 9, 1997.

[4] Ibid.

[5] Jack Olson, January 14, 1998.

[6] Captain Gerry Dawson, March 6, 1997.

[7] Ibid, February 15, 1997.

[8] Ibid, January 11, 1998.

[9] Sharon Dawson, March 17, 1997.

[10] Sharon Dawson, March 17, 1997.

[11] Jim Harding, January 10, 1998.

[12] Jack Olson, January 14, 1997.

[13] —— *Soundings*, American Steamship Company, January 1997, Vol. 16, Number 3, from a letter of appreciation to Captain Smyth, dated November 6, 1996, by Captain Trosvig, US Coast Guard Commander, Group Sault Ste. Marie.

[14] —— *Soundings*, American Steamship Company, March/April, 1997, Vol. 17, Number 1.

[15] Captain Gerry Dawson, March 11, 1997.

[16] Ibid, May 26, 1997.

[17] Sharon Dawson, December 3, 1997.

[18] Joseph Campbell, *The Hero with a Thousand Faces.* (Bollinsen Series XVII, Princeton University Press, 1993), p. 16.

[19] In part from Gene Onchulenko's program notes for the Mariners' Dinner and Dance, February 28, 1997.

[20] —— *Soundings*, American Steamship Company, March/April, 1997, Vol. 17, Number 1, p. 1.

Afterword

[1] Barry Lopez, *Arctic Dreams, Imagination and Desire in a Northern Landscape.* (Bantam Books, 1997), pp. 232-238.

[2] Peter Ostwald, *Glenn Gould, The Esctasy and Tragedy of Genius.* (New York/London, W.W. Norton, 1997) p. 232-238

[3] p.k. page, "Sufferings," *The Glass Air, Selected Poems*, (Toronto/Oxford/New York, Oxford University Press, 1985), p. 21, 1985.

Epilogue

[1] —— *Decorations for Bravery*, The Chancellery, Rideau Hall, Ottawa, Ontario. (Not dated.)

VISUAL CREDITS

All photographs appearing within this publication are the work of the author, Joan Skelton, and are used with her permission, except for those visuals listed below.

Charts in the first colour section (cs 2 & 3), created by Jim Harding and used with his permission.

Photographs:

Title page. *Grampa Woo II*. Courtesy Dana Kollars Collection.

Chapter One.

P. 2, *Walter J. McCarthy Jr.*; p. 5, The *Glenada*. Courtesy Gene Onchulenko.

P. 7, *Grampa Woo II*. Courtesy Dana Kollars Collection.

Chapter Two.

P. 25, Lake Superior seiche. Courtesy T. Virene.

Chapter Three.

P. 42, Captain Elliott Dawson; p. 44, Gerry Dawson at 3 1/2 years, and Three captains in one family. Courtesy Wealthy Dawson Collection.

Chapter Four.

P. 55, Inga Thorsteinson on the museum ship *Nonsuch*; p. 56, Inga's first boat; p. 57, The *River Rouge* on the Winnipeg River, and Marvin Thorsteinson; p. 62, Igna Thorsteinson on the *River Rouge*; p. 71, On the *Alexandria*. Courtesy Inga Thorsteinson Collection.

Chapter Five.

P. 76, The *Glenada*. Courtesy Gene Onchulenko.

P. 81, The *Rosalee D.* loading tailings. Courtesy Wealthy Dawson Collection.

Chapter Six.

P. 91, *Grampa Woo*. Courtesy Dana Kollars Collection.

Chapter Seven.

P. 120, The *Glenada*, leaving Thunder Cape; p. 123, Receiving people from the breakwall. Courtesy David Akin, *Chronicle-Journal*.

Chapter Eight.

P. 125, *Grampa Woo* impaled on rocks. Courtesy Gail Jackson, Parks Canada.

P. 127, Divers Alexander Paterson and Don Price. Courtesy Alexander Paterson Collection.

P. 131, Mesh-bottom life rafts. Courtesy Gerry Dawson Collection.

Author's photo.

P. 186, Courtesy Stan Kurisko.

Cover photographs by Joan Skelton.

GLOSSARY

Glossary of Nautical Terms

aft: Near, toward, or at the *stern* of a ship.

ballast: Bulk material carried for weight to stabilize a ship, usually water.

barge: A large cargo-carrying craft that is towed or pushed by a tug on both seagoing and inland waters.

beam: The width of a ship at its widest point.

bilge: In general, the bottom of a ship. Specifically, where the bottom meets the side of the exterior *hull*, the inside of the hull where seepage collects.

bitts: Posts on a ship's deck for tying up mooring or towing lines.

boat hook: A long wooden pole with a blunt hook on it.

bollard: A thick, low post usually of iron or steel mounted on a wharf or the like to which mooring lines from vessels are attached.

bow: The *forward* or front part of a ship.

bowsprit: A large spar that projects forward from the forward end of a ship.

bow thruster: Small *propeller* fixed sideways in ship's bow to assist with manoeuvring.

bridge: An elevated structure extending across or over the *weather deck* of a vessel, containing stations for control and visual communications.

broach: To veer or yaw dangerously so as to lie broadside to the waves. Also called "falling into the trough."

bulbous bow: Ship's *bow* forms a bulb-shape below the waterline, designed to minimize drag caused by large a bow wave.

bulk carrier or bulker: Two hundred to 1,000 foot ship designed to carry loose cargo such as coal, ore, limestone or grain, which is dumped into *holds*.

bulkhead: Any wall-like construction inside a vessel.

bulwark: The part of a ship's side that extends above the main *deck* to protect it against heavy weather.

cabin: An enclosed compartment in a ship used as shelter or living quarters.

camber: The arch or slope from side to side of a vessel's *weather deck* for water drainage. Also known as round of beam.

cleat: An object of wood or metal having one or two projecting horns to which ropes may be fastened.

clevis: Or shackle, an omega or u-shaped metal fastener for securing ropes.

clipper: A sharp-*bowed* sailing vessel of the mid-19th century, having tall *masts* and sharp lines; built for great speed.

cutter: The small powerful seaworthy patrol vessels of the Coast Guard, the term *cutter* probably handed down from the deep, narrow, fast-sailing single-masted craft used earlier.

dead-reckoning: Ship's position estimated on the basis of compass heading and forward speed, used before *GPS*, *radar*, and *loran*. Ship's position estimated without electronic devices.

deck: Horizontal or *cambered* and sloping surfaces on a ship, like floors in a building.

draw: A vessel is said to draw so many feet of water according to how much water it needs to float, the *draft*.

draft: The depth of water necessary to float a vessel.

equinox: The time when the sun crosses the plane of the Earth's equator making night and day all over the world of approximate equal length and used to mark the transition of seasons; vernal equinox about March 21, autumnal equinox about September 22. Considered a time for unusual storms.

exotics: Species that are not native to the Great Lakes and have been intentionally or accidently introduced.

eye: Loop

fetch: The extent of open water across which wind blows, one of three factors affecting wave height. The other factors are speed of the wind and length of time the wind has been blowing.

fittings: Equipment and consumable goods placed on a ship in preparation for its active service and required by its allowance list or for operation.

flotsam: Floating goods or wreckage.

following sea: Seas that move in the same direction as the boat is heading; wind blowing from astern.

fore: 1. The front part of a ship. 2. In the direction or towards the bow.

foremast: The mast nearest the *bow* of a ship.

freeboard: The distance from the top centre of the upper seaworthy deck to the water.

green sea or water: Solid water taken aboard, not foam or spray. Also called a boarding sea.

GPS (Global Positioning System): A navigation system that uses satellites to provide a receiver anywhere on Earth with extremely accurate measurements of the three-dimensions of position, velocity and time.

gross ton: Measurement of a ship's entire capacity in *registered tons*, where one ton equals 100 cubic feet of space. Registered tons are not a measure of weight.

gunwale: The upper edge of the side of a boat. The railing. Also spelled gunnel.

heel: For a ship to incline or be inclined to one side.

helm: The tiller or wheel controlling a ship's *rudder*.

hold: Portion of a ship's *hull* used for carrying and stowing cargo.

horsepower: A unit of power equal in the United States to 746 watts, nearly equivalent to the English gravitational unit of the same name that equals 550 foot-pounds of work per second.

hull: The body or shell of a ship.

immersion hypothermia: Occurs to a person immersed in cold water when heat loss from the body exceeds the capacity for heat production. There is rapid temperature decline, first in the peripheral tissues and subsequently in the core. In the early phases, death can result from cardiac arrhythmias and drowning induced by breathing irregularities, illogical behaviour, or muscular abnormalities. After ten or 15 minutes of immersion, the person feels terrible and there is intense shivering. After 15 to 20 minutes the core temperature begins to cool, shivering stops, and death likely occurs when the core temperature reaches 30 degrees C (86 degrees F). Estimated survival time ranges from one to three hours, depending on water temperature, clothing, body fat, and physical exertion. Hypothermia can occur in water as mildly cold as the low twenties Celsius (low seventies Fahrenheit). As a rule of thumb, if no-one is swimming at the beaches, a significant potential for hypothermia is present.

ketch: A sailing vessel rigged *fore* and *aft* on two masts, the larger *forward* one being the main mast and the after one, stepped forward of the rudder post being the *mizzen*.

knot: A speed unit of 1 nautical mile, about 1.15 statute miles per hour.

laker: A lake-going freighter with maximum length of 1,000 feet.

launch: A small propeller-driven boat.

lee: Sheltered or down-wind.

loran: Long-range navigation system that uses radio signals transmitted at specific times. An onboard receiver computes position by measuring the difference in time of signal reception.

mafor: A marine forecast.

master: The captain of a merchant ship.

mate: A deck officer ranking below the master on a merchant ship.

mizzen: The third mast of a vessel. A *fore* and *aft* sail. Sometimes the *aftermast* sail.

monkey fist: The weighted end of a rope used for heaving.

moor: To secure a ship by attaching it to a fixed object or mooring buoy.

moving a ship: Assistance given by one or two tugs to an ocean or lake freighter to help it manoeuvre in or out of a harbour or berth, or between loading docks. Such assistance is most often given to ocean ships. Occasionally a lake freighter requires assistance because of wind, ice or absence of *bow-thrusters*. A pilot, who directs the ship in the harbour, is only required on ocean vessels.

When berthing or assisting a vessel into an elevator or dock for loading, the bow tug approaches the vessel as it nears the entrance to the harbour. It manoeuvres alongside the ship to a position near the bow. The tug's crewman throws a coiled 3/8 inch heaving line up to the vessel's crew who pulls it aboard with the *monkey fist*, the weighted end. Attached to the other end of the heaving line is a *pennant*, a 7/8 inch steel cable 15 to 30 feet long with eyes—loops—at both ends, one attached to the heaving line, the other attached to the tug's working line, each end secured with a clevis, or shackle, a metal fastener. The working line is pulled aboard the vessel, and secured to tie-up cleats or the bow *bitt*. The working line is a three to four inch diameter eight strand polypropylene rope.

The *working line* is made fast—fastened tightly—to the bow bitt or cleat on the tug. The tug then pushes the vessel towards the dock or pulls back on the line to position the vessel closer or farther away from the dock depending on the wind and other factors as judged by the pilot or master of the ship. When the ship is tight against the dock and in position for loading, the two tugs hold the ship in position until the crew of the ship puts out its mooring lines and tightens them up. The procedure of moving a ship is variable. A less safe procedure than throwing up the tug's heaving line with pennant and working line attached is for the vessel to drop its lines down from the vessel to the tug.

When moving a vessel away from a berth or loading dock, the *eyes* of the mooring lines of the vessel are unhooked from the mooring *bollards* on the dock by linesmen. The crewman on the tug at the bow grabs the line with a *pike pole* and makes it fast to the bow *bitts* of the tug. The stern tug pushes against the ship to hold it against the dock while the bow tug steers the bow of the ship out into the main part of the harbour and manoeuvres the vessel in the direction of a breakwall exit or another berth or loading dock. Moving a ship takes between 30 minutes to six hours or more. In 1996, the cost per move ranged between $1,000 to $2,800 per tug.

nautical mile: The length of one minute of latitude on the surface of the earth. Longer than a statute mile: 6,080 feet. In navigation, 6000 feet and 2000 yards are usually used.

net tonnage: *Gross tonnage* minus the crew cabins, storerooms and machinery spaces.

northeaster: A stormy wind with waves from the northeast. Also spelled nor'easter.

northwester: A stormy wind with waves from the northwest. Also spelled nor'wester.

notship: Notice to shipping warning of a hazard.

package freighter: Ship that carries cargo that is packaged in barrels, boxes or bags, often called general cargo.

pennant: A strong steel cable with eyes at either end. Sometimes called pendant.

pike pole: A long wooden pole with a sharp metal hook on it, used as an extension of the arm and hand.

plimsol mark: Symbol marked on the side of a merchant ship to specify the maximum depth to which the vessel can be safely loaded.

pooped: Term applied when a wave breaks over the stern.

port: The side of ship that is on the left of a person facing forward.

radar: Electronic navigational device using transmitted and reflected radio waves to locate objects or shoreline features.

red fin: Lake trout with red flesh.

rail to rail: When wave action causes the railing along the sides of a ship to touch the water as the ship *heels* from side to side.

registered ton: One ton equals 100 cubic feet of space (not weight).

saltie: An ocean-going vessel.

schooner: A sailing vessel with two or more *masts* rigged *fore* and *aft*. The *foremast* is shorter than the other mast(s).

scupper: A drain at the edge of a deck exposed to the weather for allowing accumulated water to drain away into the sea or into the *bilges*.

seiche: An oscillation in water level from one end of a lake to another due to rapid changes in winds and/or atmospheric pressure. Most dramatic after an intense local weather disturbance passes over one end of a large lake.

skiff: A small light rowing boat or wherry.

spar: A long, round stick of steel or wood, often tapered at one or both ends, and usually a part of a ship's masts or rigging.

squall: A strong wind with sudden onset and more gradual decline, lasting for several minutes. A squall is reported only if a wind speed of 16 *knots* or higher is sustained for at least two minutes.

square rig: A sailing-ship *rigged* with rectangular sails set approximately at right angles to the keel line.

starboard: The side of a ship that is on the right of a person facing forward.

stem: The foremost part of a ship's *hull*.

stern: The aftermost part of a ship.

superstructure: Collective term for all parts of a vessel above the main deck. Also called upperworks.

surfman: A member of the U.S. Life Saving Service who rescued stranded crews from shipwrecks.

swamp: To fill with water to the point of sinking. Similar to water-logging.

trim: To cause a desirable position in the water by arrangement of ballast, cargo or passengers.

transom: The flat, vertical *aft* end of a boat or ship.

tug or tugboat: A powerful, strongly built boat designed to tow or push other vessels.

weather deck: The uppermost deck of a ship; any deck that does not have overhead protection from the weather.

wheel: For steering the ship, affixed to the ship's rudder. Or, slang for a ship's propeller.

wherry: A light rowboat for one or two people, originally used as a water taxi or fishing boat.

wheelhouse: A compartment on or near the bridge of a ship that contains the steering wheel and other controls, compass, charts, navigating equipment and means of communicating with the engine room and other parts of the ship. Also known as pilothouse.

working line: A heavy cable used by tugs for towing or moving a ship.

wind tide: A rise in water level due to pressure of the wind. Also, called set-up.

zebra mussel: A small freshwater mollusk that was introduced accidentally to North American waters via ballast water from a transoceanic vessel. The zebra mussel has had significant negative economic and ecological effects. It closes water intake pipes and attaches to and fouls boat hulls, dock pilings and other objects.

Zulu: A word coined to stand for Z Time. Z Time is also known as GMT (Greenwich Mean Time) or UTC (Coordinated Universal Time). Associated with Coast Guard Radio Service operation, Zulu Time is normally expressed as either a six figure group, indicating the date, hour and minute, or as a four figure group, indicating the hour and minute only. Each zone of Zulu Time requires conversion to local time. For example, in Ontario, to convert from Zulu Time to local time, subtract 5 hours during Eastern Standard Time (EST) and 4 hours during Eastern Daylight Time (EDT). A new Zulu Time day starts at 7 p.m. local time during EST, and 8 p.m. when using EDT.

Definitions adapted from:

- Barbour, A; Wildsmith, A.C.; Fairweather, F.B. Glossary: *Sailing, Rigging and Ship Building Terms*. Indian and Northern Affairs. (Not dated.)

- Bradford, Gershom. *The Mariner's Dictionary*. Weathervane Books, 1972.

- Hayler, William B., Editor in Chief. *American Merchant Seaman's Manual*. sixth edition, Centreville, Maryland, Cornell Maritime Press, 1976.

- ——— *Glossary of Nautical Terms*. University of Wisconsin Sea Grant Institute, 1996.

- Schult, Joachim. *Sailing Dictionary*, (Second Edition). Adlard Coles Nautical (London), 1992.

- ——— *The Great Lakes, An Environmental Atlas and Resource Book*. Environment Canada, United States Environmental Protection Agency, Brock University/Northwestern University, 1988.

- ——— *Webster's Encyclopedic Unabridged Dictionary*, 1996

- Wilkerson, James A; Bangs, Cameron C; Hayward, John S. *Prevention, Recognition, and PreHospital Treatment, Hypothermia, Frostbite and Other Cold Injuries*. Washington, The Mountaineers, 1986.

- Wolff Jr., Julius F. *Lake Superior Shipwrecks*: *Complete Reference to Maritime Accidents and Disasters. Lake Superior Port Cities*, 1985.

With assistance from Captain Gerry Dawson, Inga Thorsteinson, Jim Harding, Jack Olson, Brian Palmer, A/Supt. MCTS, Central and Arctic Region, and Anne Plouffe, Fisheries and Oceans, Canada.

BIBLIOGRAPHY

———— "A Field Guide to Aquatic Exotic Plants and Animals." Lake Superior Management Unit. (Not dated.)

———— "Glossary of Nautical Terms." University of Wisconsin Sea Grant Institute, 1996.

———— "Is Lake Superior's Water Quality Changing Over Time?", *Currents*. Lake Superior Center, Winter, 1997.

———— Current Status of Critical Pollutants, Lake Superior Lakewide Management Plan, Lake Superior Binational Program, 1995.

———— *Eagle Project, 7—Year Summary Report. 1990—1997.*

———— *Focus*. International Joint Commission, Special Issue on Great Lakes Areas of Concern, March/April, 1998.

———— *Guide to Eating Ontario Sport Fish*. (18th Edition revised) Ministry of Energy and the Environment, Queen's Printer, 1995-1996.

———— *Lake Sediment Studies-Thunder Bay, Lake Superior, Northern Wood Preservers Sediment Sampling Program, 1988*. Beak Consultants Ltd., and Dominion Soil Investigation Inc., Ontario Ministry of the Environment, Northwestern Region.

———— "Lake Superior 1997 Travel Map," *Lake Superior Magazine,* 1997.

———— *Northern Wood Preservers Site Remediation Plan*. Acres International Ltd. In association with Chester Environmental Ltd. Ministry of the Environment, Thunder Bay, Ontario, 1993.

———— *The Archeology of North Central Ontario, Prehistoric Cultures North of Superior*. Ministry of Culture and Recreation, 1981.

———— *The Great Lakes, An Environmental Atlas and Resource Book*. Environment Canada, United States Environmental Protection Agency, Brock University/Northwestern University, 1988.

———— *The Waters of Lake Huron and Lake Superior, Volume III (Part A), Report to the International Joint Commission by the Upper Lakes Reference Group*. 1977.

———— *Webster's Encyclopedic Unabridged Dictionary*. 1996.

———— *Prehistoric Cultures of North of Superior*. Ministry of Culture and Recreation, Historical Planning and Research Branch, 1975.

Allen, W.T.R, *Wind and Sea:* State of sea photographs for the Beaufort wind scale = *Le vent et la mer*: photographies de l'état de la mer pour l'échelle de Beaufort. (Downsview). Environment Canada, Atmospheric Environment Service, 1983.

Barbour, A; Wildsmith, A.C.; Fairweather, F.B. *Glossary: Sailing, Rigging and Ship Building Terms*. Indian and Northern Affairs. (Not dated.)

Bascom, Willard. *Waves and Beaches*. Anchor Books, Anchor Press/ Doubleday, 1980.

Bell, Howard. "Superior Pursuit, Facts about the Greatest Great Lake," *Superior Advisory Notes*. Minnesota Sea Grant Extension, University of Minnesota, 1985.

Bennett, E.B. "Characteristics of the Thermal Regime of Lake Superior," *Journal of Great Lakes Research*. 1978.

Bennett, E.B. "Climatic Normals." *Journal of Great Lakes Research*. 1978.

Bogue, Margaret Beattie and Palmer, Virginia A. *Around the Shores of Lake Superior: A Guide to Historic Sites*. The University of Wisconsin Sea Grant College Program, 1979.

Bradford, Gershom. *The Mariner's Dictionary*. Weathervane Books, 1972.

Campbell, Joseph. *The Hero with a Thousand Faces*. Bollingen Series XVII, Princeton University Press, 1973.

Carlton, James T. "Exotic Species Update: Are Ballast Water Regulations Working?" *Focus*. March/April, 1995.

Conrad, Joseph. *Lord Jim*. The Modern Library, Random House. [Not dated] Copyright 1921 by Doubleday, Doran & Co. Inc.

Dahl, Bonnie. *The Superior Way, Second Edition, A Cruising Guide of Lake Superior*. Lake Superior Port Cities, 1992.

Drew, Wayland and Littlejohn, Bruce. *Superior: The Haunted Shore*. Gage Publishing, 1975.

Hall-Armstrong, Jean. *Ballast Water: State of the Science, Guidelines and Regulations, North Shore of Lake Superior Remedial Action Plans Technical Report #21I*. 1994.

Hayler, William B., editor in chief. *American Merchant Seaman's Manual*. Sixth edition. Cornell Maritime Press, 1980.

Junger, Sebastian. *The Perfect Storm*. W.W. Norton & Co., 1997.

Lopez, Barry. *Arctic Dreams, Imagination and Desire in a Northern Landscape*. Bantam Books, 1989.

Lovelock, J.E. *Gaia, A New Look at Life on Earth*. Oxford University Press Paperback, 1991.

MacInnis, Dr. Joseph. *Fitzgerald's Storm, The Wreck of the Edmund Fitzgerald*. MacMillan Canada, 1997.

MacNeish, R.S. "A Possible Early Site in the Thunder Bay District, Ontario," *National Museum of Canada Bulletin. No. 126: 23-49*, Ottawa, 1952.

Morgan, Elaine. *The Descent of Woman*. Stein and Day Publishers, 1972.

Morgan, Elaine. *The Aquatic Ape, A Theory of Human Evolution*. Stein and Day Publishers, 1982.

Nelson, Nancy. "Clearly Superior" *Seiche*. Minnesota Sea Grant, University of Minnesota, March, 1998.

Ostwald, Peter, Glenn Gould, *The Esctasy and Tragedy of Genius*. W.W. Norton, 1997.

Pye, E.G. *Geology and Scenery, North Shore of Lake Superior*. Ontario Department of Mines, 1969.

Schult, Joachim, *Sailing Dictionary* (Second Edition). Adlard Coles Nautical (London), 1992.

Skelton, Joan. *The Survivor of the Edmund Fitzgerald*. Penumbra Press, 1985.

Smith, Wilbur. *Hungry as the Sea*. Mandarin Paperback, 1995.

Stonehouse, Frederick. *Wreck Ashore, The United States Life-Saving Service on the Great Lakes*. Lake Superior Port Cities, 1994.

Stonehouse, Frederick. *Isle Royale Shipwrecks*. Avery Color Studios, 1997.

Thurber, James. *The Thurber Carnival*. Harper & Brothers, 1945.

_____ *Toxic Chemicals in the Great Lakes and Associated Effects, Synopsis*. Environment Canada, Department of Fisheries and Oceans, Health and Welfare Canada, 1991.

Vander Wal, Jake and Watts, Paul D. eds. *Making a Great Lake Superior*. Lakehead University, Centre for Northern Studies, Occasional Paper #9, 1992.

Volgenau, Gerald. "A Superior Odyssey," *Detroit, A Special Issue*. Detroit Free Press, August 9, 1981.

Wilkerson, James A., Bangs, Cameron C., Hayward, John S., *Prevention, Recognition, and PreHospital Treament, Hypothermia, Frostbite and Other Cold Injuries*. (Washington) The Mountaineers, 1986.

Wolff, Julius F. Wolff Jr. *Lake Superior Shipwrecks, Complete Reference to Maritime Accidents and Disasters*, Lake Superior Port Cities, 1990.

INDEX

Author, Joan Skelton, near Thunder Bay, Lake Superior.

About the Author

Rescue from Grampa Woo is another contribution by Joan Skelton to the gathering lore of the Great Lakes. Rightfully, she has been included in *The Encyclopedia of Literature of the Seas and Great Lakes,* published by the University of Minnesota Press, and in *The Women's Great Lakes Reader*.

The author is an expatriate Torontonian who has adopted the near North as her home. In fact, when she first saw Lake Superior she felt she had come home.

Other works by Joan Skelton include: *Interlude: The Story of Elliot Lake* (1977) and *The Survivor of the Edmund Fitzgerald* (1985).